Revitalization: Explorations in World Christian Movements
Pietist and Wesleyan Studies
Series Editor J. Steven O'Malley

Revitalization: Explorations in World Christian Movements

This volume is published in collaboration with the Center for the Study of World Christian Revitalization Movements, a cooperative initiative of Asbury Theological Seminary faculty. Building on the work of the previous Wesleyan/Holiness Studies Center at the Seminary, the Center provides a focus for research in the Wesleyan Holiness and other related Christian renewal movements, including Pietism and Pentecostal movements, which have had a world impact. The research seeks to develop analytical models of these movements, including their biblical and theological assessment. Using an interdisciplinary approach, the Center bridges relevant discourses in several areas in order to gain insights for effective Christian mission globally. It recognizes the need for conducting research that combines insights from the history of evangelical renewal and revival movements with anthropological and religious studies literature on revitalization movements. It also networks with similar or related research and study centers around the world, in addition to sponsoring its own research projects.

It is important to acknowledge that revitalization movements inherently manifest theological diversity and even polarity – a phenomenon widely manifest in the present day. This fact underscores the importance of James Schwenk's in-depth study of the correspondence reflecting areas of disagreement between John Wesley and George Whitefield, leaders in early Methodism. How these issues were handled in the midst of a common commitment to revitalization serves to advance the research objectives of the Center.

J. Steven O'Malley
Director
Center for the Study of World Christian
Revitalization Movements
Asbury Theological Seminary

For Lore

The Road goes ever on and on
Down from the door where it began.
Now far ahead the Road has gone,
And I must follow, if I can,
Pursuing it with eager feet,
Until it joins from larger way
Where many paths and errands meet.
And whither then? I cannot say.
                           —J.R.R. Tolkien

Thank you for walking down life's road with me

Catholic Spirit

*Wesley, Whitefield, and the
Quest for Evangelical Unity in
Eighteenth-Century
British Methodism*

James L. Schwenk

*Revitalization: Explorations in
World Christian Movements
Pietist and Wesleyan Studies, No. 26*

The Scarecrow Press, Inc.
Lanham, Maryland • Toronto • Plymouth, UK
and
The Center for the Study of
World Christian Revitalization Movements
2008

SCARECROW PRESS, INC.

Published in the United States of America
by Scarecrow Press, Inc.
A wholly owned subsidiary of
The Rowman & Littlefield Publishing Group, Inc.
4501 Forbes Boulevard, Suite 200, Lanham, Maryland 20706
www.scarecrowpress.com

Estover Road
Plymouth PL6 7PY
United Kingdom

British Library Cataloguing in Publication Information Available

Library of Congress Cataloging-in-Publication Data

Schwenk, James L., 1965–
  Catholic spirit : Wesley, Whitefield, and the quest for evangelical unity in eighteenth-century British Methodism / James L. Schwenk.
    p. cm. — (Pietist and Wesleyan studies ; , No. 26) (Revitalization: explorations in world Christian movements)
  Includes bibliographical references and index.
  ISBN-13: 978-0-8108-5837-4 (pbk. : alk. paper)
  ISBN-10: 0-8108-5837-1 (pbk. : alk. paper)
  1. Christian union—Methodist Church. 2. Methodist Church—Great Britain—History—18th century. 3. Wesley, John, 1703–1791. 4. Whitefield, George, 1714–1770.
  5. Great Britain—Church history—18th century. I. Title.

BX8331.3.S39 2008
287'.5—dc22   2007038078

Table of Contents

Foreword

Much has been written about the two great leaders of the Evangelical Revival of the eighteenth century–John Wesley, the founder of Arminian Methodism, and George Whitefield, the founder of Calvinistic Methodism. Wesley and Whitefield interacted over a period of four decades, first at Oxford University, then as fellow itinerant evangelical priests in the Church of England, until Whitefield's death in 1770. Wesley, older by eleven years, did not die until 1791. Biographies and theological studies of the two have necessarily described their relationship.

Friendship between the two was strained to the breaking point over their differing views on the role of the human will in the process of salvation, Whitefield preferring the Calvinist approach and Wesley advocating human free will for all and in all by "preventing grace." While theological differences between the two are generally emphasized by those who have studied and compared them, James L. Schwenk, without minimizing their quarrels, has chosen to show places of agreement on such issues as the authority of scripture, justification by faith, and the necessity of New Birth.

Schwenk convincingly argues that both Wesley and Whitefield endeavored to forge a consensus among Christian believers of various denominations, including Anglicans, Roman Catholics, and Quakers. Both possessed "a catholic spirit" and for that reason labored to form an "evangelical catholicity." Schwenk's research opens new insights into the commonalities of their theological achievements and sheds fresh light on the eighteenth century and its contribution to our time.

Charles Yrigoyen, Jr.
Director of United Methodist Studies
Evangelical Theological Seminary

Editor's Preface

James L. Schwenk, Professor of Church History and Dean of the Chapel at Evangelical School of Theology, helps students of early Methodism understand the Wesley-Whitefield disagreements from the standpoint of their common commitment to the overarching purposes of the Evangelical Awakening, in which they were both centrally engaged. Basing his conclusions on a firsthand examination of sources, he makes the case for viewing their important correspondence from a centripetal rather than a centrifugal point of view.

That is, this discussion was conducted as part of an effort to clarify and strengthen the revival to which both were committed, despite the serious theological and stylistic differences that engaged them. That commitment meant that they were unwilling to allow those issues' divisive implications to prevail in their day. In this, they offer insight not only for scholars but also for contemporary practitioners of revitalization.

J. Steven O'Malley
Editor
Pietist and Wesleyan Studies Series

Acknowledgments

This work bears the unseen fingerprints of many who have "touched" it through their advice and support. Thanks must go to Steve Voguit, my history teacher at Wilson High School, for reminding me that history is not just dates and places, but also, people. To my earliest mentors in the study of Christian history, Leon Hynson and Robert Hower, I owe my deep respect for the British Christian tradition in general, and Wesley studies in particular. My only regret is that Leon did not live to see this work in print. Enjoy your reward, my friend. Ken Rowe and Chuck Yrigoyen further imprinted this work by helping me to think clearly and deeply about Wesley and Whitefield. Thanks must also be extended to my colleagues at Evangelical School of Theology who have touched this work through their encouragement and prayers. My deepest appreciation also extends to J. Steven O'Malley, fellow adventurer in Pietist and Methodist history, who read the original manuscript and guided me through its publication.

Christians believe that the Church, as the Body of Christ, is made up of members both on earth and in eternity. Several members of "the Church triumphant" touched this work by touching my life with their quiet example of Christian piety. I hope that Ida Finefrock, Henrietta Erdman, and Francis and Mary Schwenk are proud of this work. Their legacy, passed on to my parents, Donald and Patricia Schwenk, continues to bear fruit. Dad and Mom, you have given much. May you receive much in return.

Wesley and Whitefield depended upon each other's friendship throughout their lives and ministries. I, too, depended on friends for support, discernment, and spiritual formation. The Richland, PA LIFE Group of Community Evangelical Church has meant more to me and my family than they may ever know. Thank you, Pastor Bruce and Gloria Hill, Craig and Debbie Thompson, Scott and Michelle Brown, Dave and Fern Brenneman, Ron and Joan Steiner, and Cary and Lisa Whiteley. You helped me "step out of the boat."

Finally, the most cherished fingerprints have been left on this work by those who have sacrificed the most. Heather and Tyler Schwenk have seen more of the back of Dad's head than the front of it as he has labored over this project. Thank you for understanding when I had to work, and thank you for "interrupting me" from time to time, reminding me of what is most important in life.

And to Lore: Thank you for you love, your prayers, and your encouragement. This work is as much yours as it is mine. To you, I dedicate this book and my heart, all over again.

Chapter 1

Catholic Spirit in a Time of Change

The year 1891 marked the centennial of the death of John Wesley. Methodists around the world commemorated the event with worship experiences, dedication services, and celebrations of the life and ministry of the founder of their movement, who laid claim to the "world" as "his parish." From Methodism's inauspicious beginning at Oxford, its near-fatal Georgia experiment, and its "third birthday" on a London street called Aldersgate, Methodists in the closing decade of the nineteenth century celebrated a global movement upon which the sun never set. Yet in its early years, Methodism experienced ecclesiological and theological growing pains that could just as easily have torn it apart. The question of separation from the Church of England drove a wedge between members of the Wesley family, with Charles fighting for unity, while John saw *de facto* separation as "expedient." The theological debate between Calvinistic Methodists and Arminian Methodists resulted in divergent streams of the same movement. Either of these controversies could have destroyed the young Methodist movement, assigning it a place on what former U.S. President Ronald Reagan called "the ash-heap of history."[1]

By 1891, Methodism had fully embraced Arminian theology, and was an autonomous denomination, connected only through her history to the Church of England. Echoes of the early years of the movement and the "catholic spirit" exhibited by John Wesley and George Whitefield still resonated in the ears of some. Bevan Braithwaite sent to *The Contemporary Review* an account he received from Edward Pease, who, as a young man, heard Wesley preach in one of the Methodist chapels. As Pease related and Braithwaite retold, after Whitefield's death in 1770, several women approached Wesley with a question. Fond of both Wesley and Whitefield, and well aware of the theological debate that often accompanied their names, they queried Wesley as to whether he expected to see "dear Mr. Whitefield in heaven?" Wesley paused, and then replied with a serious tone that he did not expect to see Whitefield there. His interrogator was not surprised, indicating that she had received the answer she concluded she would hear. Wesley planned on being in heaven, and he believed Whitefield would not! But the man who often claimed to possess a "catholic spirit" quickly disavowed her of her incorrect conclusion. "Do not misunderstand me, madam; George Whitefield was so bright a star in the firmament of God's glory, and will stand so near the throne, that one like me, who am less than the least, will never catch a glimpse of him."[2]

Another episode indicates that the high regard in which Wesley held Whitefield worked both ways. Upon his death in Newburyport, Massachusetts, word was sent back to England, which led to a period of mourning on both sides

1

of the Atlantic. Although burial in his homeland proved impossible, ministers at Whitefield's Tottenham Court chapel discovered that he had hoped to be buried there. He had desired to be laid to rest in the chapel, and that his brothers in Christ, John and Charles Wesley, might be buried beside him. Prior to his last trip to America, Whitefield told the congregation at Tottenham Court, "(The Wesleys and I) will all lie together. You refuse them entrance here while living. They can do you no harm when they are dead."[3] John Wesley preached White-field's funeral sermon in the chapel over the spot Whitefield had hoped their bodies would rest.

The relationship between John Wesley and George Whitefield has provided grist for legend and fuel for theological debate. At first glance, the rift in their relationship appears to be based solely on theological differences, Whitefield the Calvinist, Wesley the Arminian. While this is undoubtedly part of the answer in explaining their differences, it is too simplistic to state unequivocally that this was the only reason for the breach. For, in essence, Whitefield and Wesley were very much alike: both were members of the Holy Club at Oxford, both were ordained into the ministry of the Church of England, both were committed to the spread of the gospel of Jesus Christ, centering their teaching and preaching on the necessity of the New Birth, both were committed to the revival of experien-tial religion, and both were steeped in the heritage of Pietism.[4] Even in their re-spective theologies, their disagreement appears to be based on emphasis rather than on glaring differences. The reason why Whitefield and Wesley's breach was so contentious has to lie deeper than the surface theological differences. Both men carried on cordial relationships with individuals from theological backgrounds far different from their own. Wesley's "catholic spirit" extended to Moravians (up until the time of the quietism controversy), members of the Church of England (the Church to which he remained faithful), even Roman Catholics, who he believed belonged to a church that retained "the living sub-stance of the Church, a residue of the authentic gospel . . . despite its anti-evangelical errors."[5] Whitefield's "catholic spirit" was no less diverse. Harry Stout argues that in the case of Pennsylvania, Whitefield appreciated the reli-gious toleration offered by the colony. "Whitefield would strive to bring them together under the banner of revival."[6] Pennsylvania offered a diverse group of religious preferences: Catholics, Jews, Quakers, Presbyterians, Lutherans, Ana-baptists. If Whitefield intended to make revival the "big tent" of the eighteenth century, and could include religious groups, many of which were far from the Calvinist fold, why did he have such a violent reaction against Arminian Metho-dism, personified by John Wesley? While theology surely played some role in the schism, the outspoken personalities of Whitefield and Wesley were the key factors. Quiet Quakers and low-key Lutherans who largely kept any differences to themselves were no threat to Whitefield, even if the differences between them were great! But an outspoken Arminian Methodist with an audience, be it in a church, the fields, or the press, gave Whitefield a target. Perhaps the strained

relationship between Whitefield and Wesley was as it was because they were so much alike; more alike than either would admit!

Given the diverse nature of their relationships with other religious groups, several questions arise. What was the "lowest common denominator," the theological foundation that had to be present in a denomination or an individual's profession for Whitefield and Wesley to continue fellowship? Were there factors, other than theological, that would foster or hinder Whitefield's and Wesley's relationship with another? Were these theological and personal factors present in the relationship between Whitefield and Wesley? Both may well have been involved in evangelical consensus-building, the quest for "evangelical ecumenicity," in eighteenth-century Methodism. While Whitefield sought to bring evangelicals together under the banner of "conversion" and Wesley sought to accomplish it under "connection," the greatest quest for evangelical ecumenism was the one involving the two great personalities of early Methodism.

If "change is inevitable," and "the only thing that remains consistent is change," it should not be surprising that the eighteenth century in Britain was marked by change. These changes were not simply causes and effects contained within the limits of the century, but rather were predicated by events reaching well into Britain's history. Civil War, the Commonwealth, the Restoration, and other events leading up to the Glorious Revolution affected England profoundly.[7] Since the church and state were so uniquely connected, it was impossible for changes in one area not to have affected the other.

The Church, indeed, was facing changes of its own. While the Church knew certain bishops of high caliber, there were those who lacked both initiative and ability. The Puritan and Non-Juring expulsions, the suppression of Convocation, the political domination of the Church, and the rise of Deistic rationalism worked together "to make prelates of the latter half of the century even less vital and less worthy than those of the former half."[8]

As religion is only one aspect of a society's makeup that both affects and is affected by the others, no study of eighteenth-century British Methodism can be complete without examining the economic, political, societal, intellectual, and religious changes that were taking place. Although John Wesley and George Whitefield were products of their age, they sought in evangelical Christianity the one constant in a dynamically changing world.

Changes in Economics

England of the eighteenth century was rapidly becoming an industrialized nation. Perhaps the economic changes evident in this era can best be described as growing pains — those experienced in a nation developing into an industrial society from an agricultural one. But while England was indeed becoming an industrial giant, and in some aspects, had already become one, over one third of the

population was still directly involved in agriculture in 1800.[9] The agricultural industry fed the developing industries in a number of ways. Sheep were raised to supply the growing wool trade. Malt was grown for the brewing process. Corn, vegetables, and dairy and beef cattle were raised to feed the nation of workers, many of whom were leaving the farming trades to enter the mines and foundries, and all too often, the squalor of the unemployed urban homeless.

The growing urban population needed to be fed from continuously shrinking farmland. The private enclosure of open land that began in the sixteenth century, while creating its own set of social dilemmas, provided a certain pragmatic justification. Centuries of use, without the benefit of crop-rotation knowledge, had caused the open corn-producing land to be leached of its fertile quality. Pasture land created by either wall or hedge allowed for livestock grazing and the added benefit of organic fertilizer. Rather than decreasing corn production by taking land out of production for a time, just the opposite was realized.[10] The introduction of the turnip into East Anglia in the mid-seventeenth century further laid the practical foundation for the feeding of livestock over the winter months. With the widespread cultivation of turnips by 1730, the higher demand for meat could be easily supplied.[11] Livestock were no longer viewed only as producers of agricultural commodities such as wool and milk, but became agricultural commodities themselves. Root crops also replenished depleted nitrogen reserves in the soil, providing an additional benefit. This allowed for fields to be kept in production, rather than lying fallow.[12] The opening of national and international markets for England's agricultural bounty encouraged a further shift from subsistence to commercial farming, designed to provide for the increasing demand for corn, beef, mutton, dairy products, and the like.[13] Other advances in agricultural theory and practice aided the burgeoning Agricultural Revolution. The introduction of double-plowing, horse-drawn cultivators, and fertilization with spread manure, lime, and marl further increased the productivity of the land.[14] The evolution of the fledgling agricultural industry was the first stage in the dawning Industrial Revolution.

The introduction of machines that could produce more goods more rapidly heralded the beginning of the Industrial Revolution. Hargreaves' "spinning jenny," Arkwright's water frame, Crompton's mule, and Cartwright's loom advanced the textile industry. Derbyshire's advances in using coal for smelting iron, Cort's discovery of coke as a replacement for charcoal in refining, and the introduction of Watt's steam engine revolutionized industry as a whole.[15] Dates for the beginning of the Industrial Revolution range from the 1740s to the 1770s, and the aforementioned inventions all appeared before, during, or after this time frame.[16] While only the earliest of these dates encompass the time of the first visible division in British Methodism, the early Methodists found themselves in the position of providing a stabilizing force in the rapidly changing era. If the Methodists were going to achieve a theological consensus, they were going to have to do it in a time when the economy of Great Britain was going through massive structural change. Many of the technological developments occurred late in the century, but sweeping economic changes were happening in what has alternately been called the "age of manufactures."[17] Improvements in agriculture, coupled with growth in the trades, produced economic expansion, higher production rates, surplus agricultural workers integrated into manufacturing, improved transportation, and a stronger financial infrastructure.[18]

As farming became more of an industry, and as cottage industry was replaced by the factory, change was inevitable for the general populace. Not only did the population grow, it was becoming increasingly less rural and more urban, with much of the populace moving from farm to town.[19] The Industrial Revolution was a boon to the economy of England, but its benefits were not shared by all. With the growth of urban areas came the growth of unemployment, poverty, and crime. Child labor was cheap and exploited to full advantage by industry. Indeed, all of England was producing food and material to support London and beyond,[20] which was also producing a sociological and economic problem for many. It was to these people of Great Britain, those affected positively or negatively by these sweeping economic changes, that John Wesley and George Whitefield brought a message of spiritual stability.

Further structural shifts took place in investment and overseas trade. Investments did not grow at staggering rates; nonetheless, investment rates grew steadily from 4% in 1700 to 8% a century later.[21] The establishment of the national debt to finance the cost of war in 1693 and the founding of the Bank of England in 1694 both laid the groundwork for the future of speculation as well as investment. While the South Sea Bubble incident undoubtedly made the more speculative investor more conservative, steady economic growth over the course of the century provided the capital for the developing Industrial Revolution.[22]

The increased production aided in the growth of overseas trade. Again, while the growth rates of trade were far from staggering, they were indeed steady. Export figures show fluctuations in the eighteenth century, but export's rise in its share of the national income of from 8% to 10% indicate its growing contribution to the economy.[23]

These changes in the British economy, while played out on the national level, affected the weavers, foundry workers, coal miners, and unemployed in places such as London, Bristol, Moorfields, and Kingswood. Developments in the national political sphere would further influence both England and her subjects.

Changes in Politics

The accession of William and Mary to the throne in 1688 ushered in a new political age in England. James II, a Roman Catholic, had been removed from the throne by Parliament, which was a move unprecedented in English history. Now the great tradition of "the divine right of kings," which declared the monarch was sovereign until abdication or death, had been unceremoniously removed by

Parliament. The Revolution proved Parliament to be more "divine" than traditional beliefs about the monarchy. The action to remove James II and enthrone William and Mary assured England of a Protestant future and heralded other changes in British politics. James II still had his supporters, and political and military maneuvers would be necessary to keep, not one, but two "Pretenders" from seizing the throne.

Parliament, armed with its newly recognized power, had achieved "the substantive acceptance of a parliamentary monarchy."[24] In the mid-seventeenth century, Cromwell dreamed of many of the realities the Revolution brought to fruition, particularly "the hegemony of the aristocracy and gentry against the threat perceived to be posed by a monarchical bureaucracy."[25] This age saw the birth of an effective Cabinet system and the position of Prime Minister. These acted as further "safeguards," as the Cabinet members had seats in Parliament and were dependent upon both Parliament and one another for the effective governance of the nation. Robert Walpole, acting as Prime Minister from 1721 to 1742, did more to establish the Cabinet system and the Premiership than any other individual. With these developments, the line between the executive and legislative bodies was considerably blurred.

The argument over royal succession was one that was not fully concluded with William and Mary's accession. More conservative elements in the Parliament would have been more comfortable with Mary's elevation to the throne with William as her Prince Consort. But the *stadtholder*[26] and Mary were enthroned, with ruling authority vested in William. Mary predeceased William, who ruled until his death in 1702, when Mary's sister Anne, a committed Tory and high-church Anglican, was coronated. With Anne's death in 1714, the Jacobite faithful saw the collapse of their last chance of James' restoration, as the royal line passed to the House of Hanover, assuring England of a Protestant future. Throughout the reigns of George I and George II, the Tory party would be out of power, and a strong Whig presence would be felt in Westminster and beyond.

This is not to suggest that the Whig "oligarchy" was unchallenged. The Jacobite uprisings of 1715 and 1745 bear witness to the challenges they faced. The "Old Pretender," James II, arrived too late and too unprepared for much to become of the uprising in 1715. Limited Catholic forces from Scotland were unable to rouse much support from their English coadjutors, and were quickly suppressed by the British military. Thus the earliest of the uprisings was ended, as much by lack of interest as by military intervention.

As the throne passed from the Stuarts to the Hanoverians, German-speaking George I was crowned king. George took several steps to assure that the Whigs would be the party in power during his reign. The Septennial Act assured that Parliamentary elections would not soon interrupt the transition. With the passage of a Universities Bill, George intended to control the awarding of Fellowships and scholarships to like-minded Whigs. The Peerage Bill of 1719 sought to limit the size of the House of Lords, providing for a Whig majority.[27] His reign also saw the selection of Robert Walpole as Prime Minister, a move that ushered in twenty years of peaceful relations abroad and less protest from the Tories at home. His one military endeavor, the naval war with Spain in 1739, proved to be the beginning of the end of Walpole's tenure as Prime Minister.

The uprising in 1745 posed a much greater threat to Whig control of Parliament and to the continuation of a Protestant monarchy. Against Walpole's judgment, England involved itself in a war with Spain, largely over the trade policies outlined in the Asiento Treaty of 1713. Not only did this involve British naval detachments aligned against Spain, but also led to land troops being sent to the Continent to again do battle with French troops in the War of the Austrian Succession. "The Young Pretender," Charles Edward, landed on the island with an opportunity to restore the House of Stuart to the throne. With royal troops occupied on the Continent, the time had come to attempt a *coup d'etat* that actually had a chance of success. Highland troops were enlisted, and the march toward London began. British troops were hastily brought home, and successfully repelled the invasion, ending the Jacobite threat. The defeat of Charles also allowed the Tory party to begin remaking itself. While it would no longer bear the suspicion of being contaminated with Jacobitism, it would not be until after the American Revolution that the Tories, under William Pitt, had recovered enough ground in Parliament to begin their own "oligarchy."

The age of the Pelhams and William (the Elder) Pitt saw, not inter-party squabbling between Tory and Whig, but intra-party wrangling between Whig party factions gathered around strong personalities. The "Old Corps," and groups faithful to the likes of Carteret, Pulteney, Lord Cobham, and the Earl of Chesterfield, had to be coalesced into a working partnership known as "Broad Bottom."[28]

The Whig coalition guided the nation through "the Forty-Five" and the administration of Prime Minister Henry Pelham. Pitt's rise to power, first under Pelham and later, in his own right, helped the nation to rally around common causes: the Revolution Settlement, the representative nature of Parliament, suspicion of Roman Catholicism, fear of threatened French expansionism, and belief in the British people, no matter what their class or faith.[29] Later, the Younger Pitt would preside over a newly designed Tory party that believed itself to be the true protector of the Revolution Settlement, and defenders, not of a democratic government, but of "a mixed constitution, mainly aristocratic, but with a popular element, and with scope left for occasional interference by the King."[30] John Wesley would use these same rallying points of nationalism, aligned with spirituality and humanism, in an attempt to provide the foundational beliefs of the developing Methodist movement.

Changes in Intellectual Life

The intellectual changes in England during the eighteenth century were no less dynamic than the economic and political changes. Among the *intelligentsia*, Cartesian philosophy was being replaced by Newtonian physics and Lockean empiricism. Locke was critical of Descartes' emphasis on abstract reason, and argued that one learns through sensory experience. Opposed to the rationalistic concept of the mind possessing innate ideas, Locke believed the mind to be a "blank tablet" on which one's experience writes its impressions throughout life. Experience supplies sensations, and from these sensations understanding allows the derivation of new and more complex ideas. Sensations and reflection on the way the mind operates on sensations are the means whereby an individual derives knowledge.[31] As the advent of Newtonian physics brought rapid changes to the world of scientific thought, so Locke's empiricism ushered in the rapidly evolving world of thought that left Descartes' rationalism behind, and introduced Berkeley's idealism and Hume's skepticism. Newton discovered that the solar system operated on a highly mechanistic system. Other thinkers suggested that the same scientific method could be applied to historical, political, and philosophical questions.[32]

Arguably, John Locke left the greatest lasting impression on the thought of eighteenth-century Britain, as his philosophy not only changed patterns of thought in the Isles, but bore fruit in the American Colonies in the thought of Jonathan Edwards and in later Revolutionary philosophy. The Kingswood colliers, shepherds of the Highlands, weavers in their cottages, and children toiling in "sweat shops" were not terribly concerned with, and probably unaware of, the writings of Locke, Berkeley, and Hume. The population in general was more concerned with meeting daily needs than with Locke's empiricism, Berkeley's idealism, or Hume's skepticism. But Wesley especially was interested in culling from the philosophers' insights into how the common person attained knowledge. Wesley believed that as individuals gained knowledge of the natural world, so they gained knowledge in the realm of the spirit. Here the epistemology of Locke and Wesley intersect.

Wesley is generally positive in his assessment of Locke: "From a careful consideration of this whole work (*Essay on Human Understanding*), I conclude that, together with several mistakes, (but none of them of any great importance) it contains many excellent truths, proposed in a clear and strong manner, by a great master both of reasoning and language."[33] Wesley supports Locke's argument that individuals have no innate ideas, and states decisively that Locke has proven his case that "all our ideas come from sensation or reflection."[34] Locke's epistemology was compatible with Wesley's evangelicalism. Just as human understanding comes through sensory perception, Wesley believed that spiritual knowledge comes through experiential means. In his abridgment of Jonathan Edwards' *A Treatise Concerning Religious Affections*, Wesley purged the Calvinism while keeping the Lockean philosophy reflected in it. Wesley emphasized faith as experience: that which is attained through spiritual senses. He noted:

> Indeed the witness of the Spirit, consists in the effect of the Spirit of God in the heart, in the implantation and exercises of grace there, and so consists in experience: And it is beyond doubt, that this seal of the Spirit is the highest kind of evidence of our adoption, that ever we obtain: But in these exercises of grace in practice, God gives witness, and sets to his seal, in the most conspicuous, eminent and evident manner.[35]

Wesley had no problem adopting contemporary intellectualism as long as it was congruent with his understanding of Scripture. Thus, throughout his ministry, Wesley stressed the possibility of knowing God through spiritual senses that were as real as physical senses. The same man who "felt his heart strangely warmed" believed wholeheartedly that others could experience the same spiritual sensation.

Other leaders of the Methodist revival were equally influenced by Lockean empiricism. Charles Wesley, whose hymns were effective in bringing the Methodist message to the common people, underscored the experiential nature of faith in many of his hymns:

> By faith we know thee strong to save
> (Save us, a present Savior thou!)
> Whate'er we hope, by faith we have,
> Future and past subsisting now.
>
> The things unknown to feeble sense,
> Unseen by reason's glimmering ray,
> With strong commanding evidence
> Their heavenly origin display.
>
> Faith lends its realizing light,
> The clouds disperse, the shadows fly;
> Th'Invisible appears in sight,
> And God appears by mortal eye.[36]
>
> How can a sinner know
> His sins on earth forgiven?
> How can my gracious Savior show
> My name inscribed in heaven?
> What we have felt and seen

> With confidence we tell,
> And publish to the sons of men
> The signs infallible.[37]

Even if allowance is made for a certain amount of poetic license, the sensate nature of the language is hard to overlook. Whitefield, too, while not as concerned about philosophical issues as were the Wesleys, nonetheless expressed the prevailing opinion concerning empirical spiritual knowledge. He queried in his sermon on conversion: "What say you to this change, dear souls? Is it not God-like, is it not divine, is it not heaven brought down to the soul; have you felt it, have you experienced it?"[38] Preaching from John 16:8, "And when he is come, he will reprove the world of sin, and of righteousness, and of judgment," Whitefield exhorted:

> The word we translate reprove, ought to be rendered convince; and in the original it implies a conviction by way of argumentation, and coming with a power upon the mind equal to a demonstration. A great many scoffers of these last days, will ask such as they term pretenders to the Spirit, how they feel the Spirit, and how they know the Spirit? They might as well ask, how they know, and how they feel the sun when it shines upon the body? For with equal power and demonstration does the Spirit of God work upon and convince the soul.[39]

While the common people may not have been interested in Locke's epistemology, several of the popular religious leaders of the day accepted Locke's theory, in understanding how the human mind achieves knowledge, both natural and spiritual. Thus the common ground between Wesley and Whitefield extended to how they understood the grace of God to be perceived in the life of the believer. They agreed on the experiential nature of true religion. Theological differences aside, Wesley and Whitefield were of the same opinion regarding the operation of spiritual sensation.

Locke's philosophy, along with the rising tide of Deism, were the staples of thought among the *intelligentsia*. Wesley may well have been interested in modern philosophy to help understand the thought processes of the masses, but for the masses, academic study in Lockean epistemology was not even considered. Grammar schools for the poor were concerned with teaching basic literacy skills. Schools for the children of aristocracy focused on practical training for future careers in business, government service, or the Church. It was not until the privileged arrived at Cambridge or Oxford that they would be exposed to loftier ideas. Even at these prestigious universities, academic standards fell, due in part to the political parceling of Fellowships and instructor appointments.[40] The "Dissenting Academies," with their emphases on modern languages, history, geography, natural science, and practical business skills, were bright spots on the educational horizon of the eighteenth century.[41]

Indeed, with the exception of the dissenting academies, there was a general secularization of intellectual thought occurring in England during this period. Attempts were being made to establish the rational basis for Christian beliefs, stripped of all their supernatural clutter. The Deists attempted to show that religion could be rationally discovered by means of natural revelation. The acceptance of natural philosophy was a spontaneous effect of a general pattern of secularization that had been at work in England for some time.[42] This increasing secularization was not confined to the regions of religion and higher learning. It incarnated itself in the moral and social conditions of the day.

Changes in Society

The interpretation of the social conditions of England in the 1700s is complicated by the seemingly positive and negative variables at work. For most of the century, England was at peace. The Agricultural and Industrial Revolutions worked together to make England the wealthiest of the European nations by the end of the century.[43] British politics had gone through a series of convulsions a century earlier, but now, both the Monarchy and Parliament had settled into a working relationship. Education had seen its brighter days, but the academic landscape was still dotted by people of the calibre of Locke, Berkeley, Smith, and Hume. In these aspects, England was becoming a fully modern country: forward in outlook, positive about what the human experience could accomplish.

Yet there was a darker side to the prosperity, what Piette called "a frightful seepage in English moral life."[44] Slave-trading helped make England a leader in world trade. The rapidly developing urban areas, while centers of commerce, also became centers of poverty. Gambling was a favorite pastime for the nobility, with wagers placed on most any pending event. "Taking a chance" could mean taking out an insurance policy on another person's life.[45] The theater, another popular diversion, was largely degraded. Whitefield preached against its evils, perhaps in reaction to his early predilection for the stage and the continuing competition it provided for his dramatic persona. "You go to plays," Whitefield exhorts, "And what do you see there! . . .When you see the players on the stage, you see the devil's children grinning at you."[46] Wesley, while less vocal in his opposition to the stage, wrote to "The Mayor and Corporation of Bristol" to discourage the building of a new playhouse.[47] Inexpensive gin appeared in the 1720s and quickly became a beverage of choice, knowing no socio-economic boundaries.[48] Crime blossomed in the seedbed of poverty and alcoholism. When captured, criminals were obliged to pay a high price: imprisonment for lesser charges, capital punishment for more serious violations. Numbering more than 150, capital crimes ranged from minor offenses to murder.[49] Treatment of the incarcerated was often inhumane. Debtors shared prison space with hardened criminals. As early as 1729

Wesley was visiting prisons as a member of the Oxford "Holy Club." This became a regular part of his ministry, and he became an observer of prison conditions, and a voice for prison reform.[50] In 1745, Wesley described Ludgate and Newgate Prisons as "dark and dreary . . . unhealthy and unclean . . . void of all that might minister comfort."[51] A visit to Marshalsea Prison in February 1753 led him to call it "a nursery of all manner of wickedness . . . a picture of hell upon earth!"[52] Wesley was not alone in his assessment of prison conditions. John Howard visited prisons in England and on the Continent, deploring the miserable treatment of prisoners.[53]

Granting that the observations of leaders of reform movements tend to paint the opposition in the darkest possible hues, there was a definite disparity between the benefits of the eighteenth century and the baneful consequences that haunted the populace. Historically, the Church has had a mixed record in responding to social issues in a positive way. But the Church in eighteenth-century England was confronted not only by questions of social morality, but also by serious questions concerning theology, intellectualism, and the Church's relevance to a rapidly changing society.

Changes in British Christianity

"True honor, though it be a different principle from religion, is that which produces the same effects."[54] Such was the attitude of much polite society. The "spirit of a gentleman, and the spirit of religion" were viewed as compatible, "the Christian ideal, above all, validated the model of a homogeneous, hierarchical society, a unitary and confessional State."[55] Clark quotes Archdeacon Paley's observation as representative of the spirit of the age: men were governed by three codes, "The Law of Honor," "The Law of the Land," and "The Scriptures," in that order.[56] Issues of personal enjoyment, making a profit, and new intellectual vistas were confronting the privileged. The urban clergy, as part of the upper class, were challenged by the same issues. The general population, while not as preoccupied with "living the good life" as they were simply with "living," were also members of the Church of England. The Church was called upon to meet the needs of both classes. It seemed ill-prepared to meet the spiritual needs of either. This is not to suggest that the entire leadership of the Church of England was apostate. There were faithful shepherds within the Anglican Church, the dissenting bodies, and the emerging Methodist movement. But with economic, industrial, political, and societal change occurring at such rapid rates, the church, especially the established Church, was in danger of being left behind.[57] Wesley, Whitefield, and the Methodists seized the opportunity, and offered stability in spirituality that could see adherents through the changing times.

Changes Within the Church of England

The Glorious Revolution was intended to ensure a Protestant future for the British people. The crowning of William and Mary itself brought change to the religious complexion of England. William, albeit a Protestant, was a Dutch Calvinist who proved to be a believer in religious toleration. Mary, while an Anglican, was not the regent. Despite the mixed Protestant pedigree of the king and queen, most of the clergy of the Church of England accepted their rule by taking the oath of allegiance. A significant minority refused to swear their allegiance to those they saw as violating the law of hereditary succession. These "non-jurors," led by Archbishop of Canterbury William Sancroft and Thomas Ken, Bishop of Bath, found themselves suspended and eventually deprived of their livings. Ken continued to attend public prayers, as he saw himself to be a faithful son of the Church. Sancroft, more determined to carry out the powers with which he believed himself rightly vested, took steps to sustain a non-juring episcopate. He died before the consecration of sympathizing bishops took place, thus the outward schism was averted, while internal problems continued.[58]

Concurrently within the Church of England, there existed the sometimes exaggerated, but nevertheless real presence of Roman Catholic sympathizers. Like the non-jurors, the Jacobites believed James II to be the legitimate heir to the throne, and his return as rightful heir and Roman Catholic believer would make England a Catholic nation once again. The Act of Toleration (1689) extended a certain amount of religious freedom to Protestant non-conformists, but not to Roman Catholics, who were now viewed as enemies of the state. The "declaration of fidelity" in the Act of Toleration states in part that the subscriber "declare(s) that no foreign (prince, person), prelate, state or potentate hath or ought to have any power, jurisdiction, superiority, preeminence or authority ecclesiastical or spiritual within this realm."[59] Catholics who had sworn allegiance to the Pope were viewed as dangerous, probably subversive, elements. The non-jurors, while sharing the Jacobites' belief in James as rightful monarch, did not share their fidelity to Rome, though they were often accused of Jacobite leanings. The Jacobite uprisings of 1715 and 1745 did little to quiet the accusations.

Members of the High Church Party were often suspected of Jacobite tendencies. Fully committed to the cherished traditions of the Church of England, the High Churchmen generally disliked the consequences of the Glorious Revolution, and maintained their loyalty to the House of Stuart.[60] "Most of them were Tories, a few were Jacobites, and none had much faith in a constitutional monarchy."[61] Unable to support the "occasional conformity" of Dissenters who would receive communion in the Church of England as a means of circumventing the Test Act of 1673, the High Churchmen made an unsuccessful attempt to close the loophole early in Anne's reign. They won a moral victory with the restoration of Convocation in 1700, but its call for "one Christian realm, exercising moral and spiritual authority over the Church through the clergy, reinforced by the legislative sanctions of a Christian parliament," while lofty, called for concessions that could not be made in the rapidly evolving cultural context.[62] The Convocations were silenced for more than a century. The High Churchmen successfully passed the Occasional Conformity Act, which prevented practicing Dissenters from holding office. Another High Church victory, the Schism Act, precluded the Dissenters from having their own schools.

The Latitudinarians were a favorite target of the High Church Party. While also fond of tradition, and seeking a return to the simple Christianity of the ancient Church, the Latitudinarians were not as doctrinaire as the High Churchmen. They looked back to the early church, "nor is there any point in divinity which is most ancient doth not prove the most rational, and the most rational, the ancientest."[63] They might well be called the "moderates" of the changing religious scene in Britain. As members of the established Church, they defended the Thirty-Nine Articles, the Constitution, and the liturgy, but found it difficult to support "passive obedience" to the hereditary monarch. Their allegiance to William and Mary marked them as dangerous in the eyes of the High Church Party, and they were further suspect due to their quest to find a middle ground between the Dissenters on the left and the High Church Party on the right. In the wake of the Restoration and Revolution, the Latitudinarians, tired of the religious controversies that were involved, sought relief for themselves and the Church through reason and practical Christianity.[64] If the Latitudinarians viewed themselves as the "moderates" between the High Church Party and the Dissenting bodies, the majority of clergy within the Church of England perceived themselves simply as the "moderates" between Roman Catholics and Protestants.[65]

Yet even their attempts to bring consensus within the Church of England were ineffective. Non-conformity also had a treasured heritage it intended to defend. Non-conformity and other theological issues endangered a united Church of England.

The Dissenting Tradition

The "Dissenting tradition" has a long, storied history in England. Since the English Reformation, there had been those who, for conscience's sake, had distanced themselves from the Church of England. During the seventeenth century, the characteristics of organized dissent became much clearer and strategically ordered. Whether they called themselves Puritans, Baptists, Presbyterians, or Quakers, the Dissenters were bound together by a common belief that the Christian life could best be lived outside of the Church of England. Dissenters in Wesley's England could point back to the previous century, to Cromwell, the epitome of a true Dissenter. While all would not agree with his politics nor his religious beliefs, one belief they held in common: mistrust and distaste for Roman Catholics and Anglicans.[66]

The Interregnum was the zenith of Puritan Calvinism in England. With the Restoration, the prominence of religious dissent began to wane for a time. Not only were devout Anglicans returning to seats in Parliament, but they were also taking steps to assure that what had happened in recent history would not happen again. The passage of The Act of Uniformity in 1662 was designed to welcome all but the most intransigent of Dissenters back into the fold. Parliament was not so naive as to believe that the implementation of such a statute would end dissent, but the law was worded so as to please the Anglican faithful, and yet not be so partisan that moderate Dissenters could not subscribe. The "times of the late unhappy troubles" had "led into factions and schisms, to the great decay and scandal of the reformed religion of the Church of England." Times had changed again, and the Act announced that the time had come "for settling the peace of the Church, and for allaying the present distempers."[67] Essentially, the Act simply called for the "reestablishment" of the Church of England as the national Church, "reinforced the position of the Thirty-nine Articles as the only statement of faith, and of the Book of Common Prayer as its expression in worship."[68] Those unwilling to subscribe were forced from the Church of England. The Act of Uniformity and the later Test Act also guarded the nation from Catholicism, which was viewed as a constant threat.

The Glorious Revolution established Protestantism as the state religion of England, and with the accession of a Dutch Calvinist king to the throne, Dissenters envisioned a hopeful future. The Toleration Act of 1689 assured that, while the Anglican Church would be the national church, those that could not abide by its worship standards and discipline would know some toleration. Far from establishing wide-ranging freedom of worship, the Act accepted the fact that one could be a loyal subject without being a member of the Church of England.[69]

The Toleration Act called for Dissenters to swear loyalty to the crown and belief in the basic Christian doctrines of the Trinity and the inspiration of the Scriptures. Dissenters who subscribed to these premises and whose meeting places were registered were allowed a degree of religious freedom. The era of religious toleration was short-lived, however, as the Occasional Conformity Act and the Schism Act were passed by the Tory-controlled Parliament in 1711 and 1714. The first disqualified Dissenters from holding public office if they, after receiving the sacrament in the Church of England, attended worship at a Dissenting meeting house. The Schism Act was designed to eliminate dissent within a generation, by closing non-conformist schools, or by replacing Dissenting teachers with those willing to teach the Anglican catechism.[70] Both acts were repealed during the reign of George I, and non-conformity was infused with new vigor with the onset of the Evangelical Awakening.

Theological Issues

The theological issues affecting the Church of England of the eighteenth century went far beyond the basic doctrinal differences between the Anglicans, Roman Catholics, and Calvinist Dissenters. The Test Act guarded against Roman Catholic influences. The Act of Uniformity and the Toleration Act, while granting limited religious freedom to Dissenters, allowed for the Church of England to gauge the extent of religious non-conformity. Other theological issues were influencing the established Church, not from without, but from within. Deism challenged the Church to examine the very rationale of its being. Rejecting revelation, the Deists sought to carry the scientific and philosophical spirit of the age into the religious realm. Generally believed to have had its beginnings in the thought of Lord Herbert of Cherbury, Deism accepted the belief in a "Supreme Deity" who is to be worshipped, the chief part of which is virtuous living. Humans are responsible to repent of wrongdoing, and can expect to be rewarded or punished after death in relation to their behavior while alive.[71] The Deists argued that these principles could be easily derived from rational reflection on nature and personal experience. There was no need for belief in supernatural revelation. The titles of the seminal Deistical works reveal this presupposition: Locke's *Reasonableness of Christianity* (1695), Toland's *Christianity Not Mysterious* (1696), and Tindal's *Christianity as old as the Creation* (1730). Toland clearly stated his goal, "Showing that there is nothing in the Gospel contrary to Reason, nor above it: and that no Christian Doctrine can be properly called a Mystery."[72] Tindal similarly asserts, that while he cannot deny the existence of revelation, that "natural and revealed religion . . . must, 'like two tallies, exactly answer one another'"[73] All agreed that "the unassisted reason of man is abundantly able to discover the few and simple truths of which genuine religion consists."[74] Butler's *Analogy* (1736), Berkeley's *Alciphron* (1732), and Law's *The Case for Reason* (1731) endeavored to defend Christianity as rational while arguing for the necessity of divine revelation, but Deism was a theology not easily discredited. Rupp summarizes the Deists' appeal:

> To a remarkable extent, western unbelief had always been conditioned by the Christian world to which it has been opposed . . . . Some of the Deists were nearer than others to Christian orthodoxy. Most of them believed in God, as supreme governor of the universe, and accepted a moral law, while some of them . . . believed in an after life and final judgment. They rejected miracles, and the "proofs" from prophecy, and particular providences. To a man they were anti-clerical. Their strength was their belief in toleration and the right of free enquiry, and this was the more admira-

ble because Christian intolerance could still make itself felt in nasty and physical ways.[75]

"The curse of eighteenth century intellectualism was not its common sense, but its lack of anything more dynamic."[76] The logic of rationalism and the ability of calm reason to discover the truths of religion in natural revelation may have appealed to the "head" while doing little for the "heart." In noting that the Church of England played an "integral part" in the "civilizing work" of the century, Trevelyan notes two major weaknesses of the Church's agenda: the discouragement of all forms of zeal, and its general neglect of the poor.[77] It was left for another movement to "stand in the gap." That movement arose from within the Church of England, and while finding it impossible to remain a reform movement from within, the Methodist movement helped provide stabilization in rapidly evolving eighteenth-century England. The Methodist movement was in part a necessary component of the changes taking place in England, and was also affected by the changing context. Methodism, like society at large, had to mature with the transforming culture. Conversely, the Methodist movement may never have developed had it not been for the intellectual, economic, theological, and societal "revolutions" that had changed England's complexion. A reform movement from its inception, Methodism's goal was to bring about remedies to the Church's defects from within. Wesley not only believed that Methodism was the "religion of the Bible and the Primitive Church," but also that it was the "religion of the Church of England," as contained in its liturgy and homilies.[78]

While the Methodists would eventually find separation from the Church of England necessary, the key leaders of the movement, John Wesley and George Whitefield, never renounced their Episcopal ordination, and remained members of the Church of England all their lives. Both Wesley and Whitefield were influenced by non-conformity. Wesley's parents both had Dissenting fathers. Susanna and Samuel Wesley eventually turned from their Dissenting heritage to find a home within the Anglican fold. To suggest that John Wesley inherited "Dissenting blood" from his ancestry is a romantic notion. If nothing else, he acquired the Wesley and Annesley predilection for standing firm in one's beliefs. Whitefield's connection with non-conformity came as a result of his reading of Scripture. While he nurtured relationships with Howell Harris, Jonathan Edwards, and other noted Calvinists, Whitefield claimed that, "I embrace the Calvinistic scheme, not because Calvin, but Jesus Christ has taught it to me."[79] Many Anglican pulpits would be closed to Wesley and Whitefield, but they found within the generally tolerant nature of the Church a theological basis centered on their affirmation of the Thirty-Nine Articles. Whitefield wrote in 1739 that he had not been accused of teaching anything contrary to the doctrine of the Church of England, and that he endeavored to "keep close to her Articles and Homilies."[80] Two weeks later he penned, "so long as I think the Articles of the Church of England are agreeable to Scripture, I am resolved to preach them up without either bigotry or party zeal."[81]

Wesley believed the Church of England to be "nearer the scriptural plan than any other in Europe," and made significant use of the Articles in his writings.[82] Wesley and Whitefield were proponents of experiential religion. Wesley emphasized the importance of spiritual sensation; Whitefield spoke to the passions. The legacy of Wesley and Whitefield lies not in how they were influenced by the eighteenth century, although an understanding of the societal context is important to understanding their lives. Wesley and Whitefield empowered their generation with innovations necessary for a renewed church, and left that legacy to the Church of succeeding generations. They reemphasized the importance of vital, "warmhearted" religion, as opposed to cold, rationalistic religion. They called the Church back to important social ministries that had been largely neglected. They also provided a paradigm of evangelical ecumenicity, whereby evangelicals could work toward consensus-building, even though doctrinal and personal differences may not be completely rectified.

During this era of major societal change, the strength of the early Methodist movement is evident. It provided spiritual, emotional, even physical and financial stability for common people who were in danger of being left in the wake of the dynamic shifts that were taking place at every level of society. But if Methodists provided a firm foundation upon which people could place their hopes for the present and the future, that stability hid a latent danger. If the united front of Methodism could be shaken, where could people turn for constancy amid change? A deteriorating relationship between the key leaders of Methodism would provide rhetoric for the "spin doctors" of the age, and serve as an indicator that Christianity did not hold out the promise for the betterment of people's lives or souls. Wesley and Whitefield's broken relationship would simply have provided a contemporary snapshot of the deterioration of the rest of society. Both men worked feverishly to prevent that from happening.

Notes

1. Ronald Reagan, "Address to Members of the British Parliament, June 8, 1982." www.reagansheritage.org/reagan/html/reagan06_08_82.shtml.

2. Methodist Preacher, *John Wesley the Methodist: A Plain Account of His Life and Work* (New York: Methodist Book Concern, 1903), 168.

3. Roy Hattersley, *The Life of John Wesley: A Brand from the Burning* (New York: Doubleday, 2003), 328.

4. I am employing here a general definition of the word "Pietism," more in line with Mark Noll's recent definition of it as a Continental Christian movement that possessed "a growing attention to the inner life of faith." Wesley and Whitefield both read the classic Pietist authors (Arndt, Spener, Franke, et al.), and Wesley edited and republished many of their ideas. For this work, however, I am employing "Pietism" in a less technical sense, to highlight its congruence with evangelicalism. As Noll suggests, "Puritanism, Pietism and evangelicalism were joined closely as analogous religious movements. Chief among their similarities was the common conviction that God could actually, actively and almost tangibly transform repentant sinners who put their trust in him." Mark Noll, *The Rise of Evangelicalism: The Age of Edwards, Whitefield, and the Wesleys* (Downers Grove, IL: InterVarsity Press, 2003), 65.

5. Albert Outler, ed., *John Wesley* (New York: Oxford University Press, 1980), 351.

6. Harry Stout, *The Divine Dramatist: George Whitefield and the Rise of Modern Evangelicalism* (Grand Rapids: Eerdmans Publishing Co., 1991), 89.

7. Gordon Rupp, Introductory Essay in *A History of the Methodist Church in Great Britain*, ed. by R.E. Davies and E.G. Rupp (London: Epworth Press, 1965), xix.

8. J. Wesley Bready, *England Before and After Wesley* (London: Hodder and Stoughton, 1938), 53.

9. William J. Hausman, "The British Economy in Transition, 1742-1789," in *British Politics and Society from Walpole to Pitt, 1742-1789*, ed. Jeremy Black (London: Macmillan Education Ltd., 1990), 62.

10. George Roy Porter, *English Society in the Eighteenth Century* (Hammondsworth, England: Penguin Books, 1982), 220.

11. Ibid., 221.

12. Ibid., 221.

13. John Morrill, "The Stuarts," in *The Oxford History of Britain*, ed. Kenneth O. Morgan (Oxford: Oxford University Press, 1988), 333.

14. Porter, 221. While Thomas Coke's estate became an agricultural showcase for advances in fertilization, other landowners, including the Townshends and Walpoles, had been experimenting with crop rotation, manure fertilization, and root crop production since the early 1700s.

15. Christopher Harvie, "Revolution and the Rule of Law," in *Oxford History of Britain*. Hausman quotes David S. Landes, who notes, "The innovations came in a sequence of challenge and response, in which the speed-up of one stage of the manufacturing process placed a heavy strain on the factors of production of one or more other stages and called forth innovations to correct the imbalance." In Hausman, 71.

16. Ibid., 54.

17. Roy Porter, "English Society in the Eighteenth Century Revisited," in *British Politics and Society from Walpole to Pitt*, 38.

18. Ibid., 38.

19. Paul Langford, "The Eighteenth Century," in *The Oxford History of Britain*, 477.

20. Daniel Defoe, *A Tour Through the Whole Island of Great Britain* (Middlesex, UK: Penguin Books Ltd., 1971), 45. Part of Defoe's stated purpose for writings of his tours through Great Britain is: ". . . not (to) forget the general dependence of the whole country upon the city of London, as well for the consumption of its produce as the circulation of its trade."

21. Hausman, 62.

22. During the reign of King George I, the South Sea Company was charged to help re-pay the national debt left over from Queen Anne's war with France. By 1720, the company sought to cut the national debt of £50 million by more than 50%. The promised dividends were attractive, and the price of company stock rose from £100 to £130 within the first four months of 1720. By July, the price per share exceeded £1,000. Throughout the autumn months, investors went on a selling spree, and "the crash was even faster than the rise." Lives and political careers were ruined. John Cannon and Ralph Griffiths, *The Oxford Illustrated History of the British Monarchy* (Oxford: Oxford University Press, 2000), 467.

23. Ibid., 63.

24. Porter, 401.

25. J.C.D. Clark, *English Society, 1688-1832.* (Cambridge: Cambridge University Press, 1986), 6-7.

26. The term *stadtholder* refers to William of Orange's hereditary position as Head of State in the Netherlands.

27. Langford, "The Eighteenth Century," 411.

28. Ian R. Christie, "The Changing Nature of Parliamentary Politics, 1742-1789," in *British Politics and Society from Walpole to Pitt*, 102.

29. George Macaulay Trevelyan, *History of England* (New York: Longmans, Green, and Co., 1928), 542.

30. Ibid., 560.

31. Robert C. Solomon and Kathleen M. Higgins, *A Short History of Philosophy* (New York: Oxford University Press, 1996), 195.

32. Herbert Butterfield, "England in the Eighteenth Century," in *A History of the Methodist Church in Great Britain*, 31.

33. John Wesley, *Works, Vol. XIII* (Peabody, MA: Hendrickson Publishing Co., 1991), 464.

34. Ibid., 456.

35. Richard E. Brantley, "The Common Ground of Wesley and Edwards," *Harvard Theological Review* 83, no. 3 (1990): 286.

36. Oliver A. Beckerlegge and Franz Hilderandt, eds., *Works of John Wesley, Vol. 7: A Collection of Hymns for the use of the People Called Methodists* (Oxford: Clarendon Press, 1987), 194-195.

37. Ibid., 195.

38. Clyde E. Fant, Jr., and William M. Pinson, Jr., *20 Centuries of Great Preaching: Wesley to Finney, Vol. 3* (Waco, TX: Word Books, 1971), 141.

39. John Gillies, *Memoirs of George Whitefield* (Hartford, CT: Edwin Hunt, 1843), 391. The sermon is titled, "The Holy Spirit Convincing the World of Sin, Righteousness, and Judgment."

40. Clark, 152-153. Clark suggests the political explanation for the academic malaise, while also noting that "much of the torpor which seems evident in retrospect reflects only

the irrelevance of the preoccupations of the late-scholastic mind to subsequent problems."

41. Rupp, 174-177. Charles Morton's second academy at Newington Green exemplified this diverse educational system. This academy was home to a garden, bowling green, "and some not inconsiderable rarities with an air pump, thermometers, and all sorts of mathematical instruments." Morton taught logic, the arts and sciences, and political science, and instructed partially in English, as opposed to the Continental style of lecturing totally in Latin.

42. C. John Sommerville, *The Secularization of Early Modern England: From Religious Culture to Religious Faith* (New York: Oxford University Press, 1992), 163. Sommerville notes how changes in British culture ". . . made an entirely naturalistic philosophy possible. The secularization of time made possible a more secular history. The secularization of the person and social relations allowed a secular social theory. Secularization of power prompted secular political theories. Secularized space was necessary to the new natural philosophy or science. And the secularization of language and of literature encouraged a secular education. All of these, in turn, would give support to theories of religion, which marks the final stage of a secularization of culture."

43. Edward P. Cheyney, *Modern English Reform: From Individualism to Socialism* (New York: A.S. Barnes and Company, 1962), 1.

44. Maximin Piette, *John Wesley in the Evolution of Protestantism* (New York: Sheed and Ward, 1937), 110.

45. Porter, 255.

46. Stout, *The Divine Dramatist*, 239. Stout quotes a sermon Whitefield preached at Long Acre, Lockington, a "fashionable street adjacent to the theatre district."

47. John Wesley, *Works, Vol. XII* (Peabody, MA: Hendrickson Publishing Co., 1991), 128.

48. Porter, 235. See also A. Skevington Wood, *The Burning Heart* (Minneapolis: Bethany Fellowship, Inc., 1978), 10. Wood quotes from *The Poetical Works of George Crabbe*, indicating the widespread use of alcohol. Crabbe satirizes "the staggering peer, the humbler pensioner, the slow-tongued bishop, the easy chaplain, and the convivial vicar."

49. Langford, 436. Wood also notes the inordinate number of capital crimes. See Wood, 11 (n. 5).

50. W. Reginald Ward and Richard P. Heitzenrater, eds., *The Works of John Wesley: Journal and Diaries, Vol. 18* (Nashville: Abingdon Press, 1988), 124.

51. Gerald R. Cragg, ed., *The Works of John Wesley: The Appeals, Vol. 11* (Oxford: Clarendon Press, 1975), 241.

52. W. Reginald Ward and Richard P. Heitzenrater, eds., *The Works of John Wesley: Journal and Diaries, Vol. 20* (Nashville: Abingdon Press, 1991), 444.

53. Porter, 306.

54. Clark, 106. Quoting *The Gentlemen's Library: Containing Rules for Conduct in all Parts of Life,* 5th ed. (London, 1760).

55. Ibid., 93.

56. Ibid., 115.

57. The Church was further hampered by having to secure the approval of a disinterested Parliament for all changes and reforms.

58. Gordon Rupp, *Religion in England, 1688-1791* (Oxford: Clarendon Press, 1986), 11-12.

59. Gerald Bray, ed., *Documents of the English Reformation* (Minneapolis: Fortress Press, 1994), 575.

60. Rupp, 54.

61. J.R.H. Moorman, *A History of the Church in England* (London: A.C. Black, 1986), 269.

62. Rupp, 63.

63. Ibid., 31. Rupp quotes a letter by "S.P.," commonly attributed to Simon Patrick, who published the earliest account of the Latitudinarians in 1662.

64. Moorman, 255.

65. Rupp, 84.

66. Rupp, 105. Rupp traces the growth of separatist doctrines to the reigns of Elizabeth and James I, where separatists inveighed against "a mixed and Established Church, against bishops, and against the liturgy."

67. Bray, 548.

68. Ibid., 547.

69. Ibid., 571.

70. Trevelyan, 500.

71. Rupp, 261.

72. Ibid., 262. Rupp quotes from the title page of Toland's *Christianity Not Mysterious*.

73. Sir Leslie Stephen, *History of English Thought in the Eighteenth Century, Vol. 1* (New York: Harbinger Books, 1962), 116.

74. Ibid., 116.

75. Rupp, 277.

76. Bready, 40.

77. Trevelyan, 519.

78. Albert C. Outler, ed., *The Works of John Wesley: Sermons, Vol. 3* (Nashville: Abingdon Press, 1986), 586. From a sermon preached at the laying of the foundation of the City Road Chapel.

79. Arnold A. Dallimore, *George Whitefield: God's Anointed Servant in the Great Revival of the Eighteenth Century* (Wheaton, IL: Crossway Books, 1990), 69.

80. George Whitefield, *Journals* (Carlisle: Banner of Truth Trust, 1992), 250.

81. Ibid., 256.

82. John Wesley, *Works, Vol. XIII*, 146. Quoted from a letter (DCCCXCII) to Sir Harry Trelawney. Wesley quoted extensively from the Thirty-Nine Articles in his *A Farther Appeal to Men of Reason and Religion*.

Chapter 2

Catholic Spirit: The Quest for Common Ground

George Whitefield and John Wesley have been historically linked to two different "streams" of the Evangelical Awakening: Whitefield to the Calvinist stream, Wesley to the Arminian Methodist. Taken at face value, this is a plausible generalization. Rarely, however, have either of these leaders of the revival been labeled as theologians. Whitefield, arguably the more popular of the two, judged solely on their preaching ability, has been nicknamed the "Grand Itinerant," and has been assessed by historians to have been the most popular orator of his day.[1] Wesley knew obvious success in his ministry as well, but is normally regarded more as the great organizer of Methodism than for charismatic preaching. While Wesley was more of a theologian than Whitefield, neither thought it necessary to leave a written systematic theology as a legacy.[2]

Upon a cursory study, it appears that Whitefield and Wesley differed widely in their theological outlook. Yet this conclusion is misleading. Both men agreed that men and women are lost in sin, stand in need of a Savior, and that only through the work of Christ accomplished on the cross can they be justified. Unfortunately, much of the scholarly work that addresses the relationship between Whitefield and Wesley focuses on the apparent theological differences that existed. It cannot be overlooked that both men carried on warm relationships with people with whom they differed widely. Both claimed to possess a "catholic spirit": the willingness to nurture relationships with those who differed in "opinions," while agreeing in the "essentials." Theologically, they were more in agreement than their followers would care to admit.

Whitefield and Wesley on Original Sin

Throughout his ministry, Whitefield confessed to a firm belief in the truth of Calvinistic theology. He maintained his convictions came, not from reading Calvin, but "from Christ and his apostles; I was taught them of God."[3] Of the doctrines of grace, Whitefield wrote,

> I am more and more convinced that they are the truths of God; they agree with the written word and the experience of all the saints in all ages: Nothing more confirms me in the belief of them, than the opposition that is made against them by natural men. Election, free grace, free justification without any regard to works foreseen, are such paradoxes to carnal minds, that they cannot away with them.[4]

Whitefield employed three components of the "Wesleyan Quadrilateral," namely Scripture, tradition, and experience, to defend his Calvinistic theology.

Whitefield defended the classic doctrines of Calvinism as central to his ministry. The "doctrines of grace" thundered from his pulpit and permeated his writings. An examination of the sermons and writings evidences Whitefield's adherence to the standard Calvinistic beliefs of original sin, regeneration, justification by faith in Christ, the final perseverance of the saints, and eternal, unconditional election.[5] These he defended as Scriptural, yet not all needed to be present for Whitefield to extend the hand of fellowship.

Wesley was not a Calvinist, but ably captured the close correlation between many Arminian Methodist beliefs and classic Calvinism. In the *Minutes of Some Late Conversations Between The Rev. Mr. Wesleys and Others*, dated August 1, 1745, a question is raised: "Does not the truth of the gospel lie very near both to Calvinism and Antinomianism?" Answering that gospel truth comes to within a "hair's breadth" of both, Wesley's elaboration in regard to Calvinism is enlightening. He contended that "the truth of the gospel" comes to the very edge of Calvinism: "In ascribing all good to the free grace of God. In denying all natural free-will, and all power antecedent to grace. And, in excluding all merit from man; even for what he has or does by the grace of God."[6] Indeed, Wesley was over-simplifying the similarities between the two camps. Both Arminian Methodists and Calvinists believed in the "free grace of God" and the denial of "natural free will," but these undoubtedly were defined differently by each side. When Whitefield spoke of the inability of individuals to respond to God's grace by faith until effectively called by God, he was speaking in terms of election. When Wesley spoke of "denying all power antecedent to grace," he was speaking of prevenient grace. Both may have used the same words, but the presuppositions behind them were completely different. Further, both Whitefield and Wesley agreed on the necessity of the New Birth and that individuals are justified by faith in the finished work of Christ. Again, viewed in light of the terms employed, both men were in complete agreement. But where Whitefield would invite his hearers by saying, "Perhaps God has called you," Wesley would say, "Whosoever will may come."

Perhaps the foundational doctrine upon which Whitefield's whole theology was based was the doctrine of original sin. It is foundational in the sense that if humanity has any residual goodness, individuals could believe that they have some role to play in saving themselves. Whitefield would allow for no usurpation of God's power in his *ordo saludis*. Thus he believed that there was nothing in human beings to merit God's grace, nor any ability within the race to do anything, even exercise faith, without God's initiation. Humanity had fallen that far. In his sermon "The Method of Grace," Whitefield decried "fine reasoners" who "pretend to say there is no such thing as original sin; they will charge God with injustice in imputing Adam's sin to us; although we have got the mark of the beast and of the devil upon us, yet they tell us we are not born in sin." The picture he paints of the human condition is morose. "If we look inwardly, we shall see enough of lusts, and man's temper contrary to the temper of God. There is pride, malice and revenge, in all our hearts; and this temper cannot come from God; it comes from our first parent, Adam, who, after he fell from God, fell out of God into the devil."[7] Whitefield fully accepted as fact that Adam's sin was "imputed" to the human race, noting that "the disobedience of our first parents was made ours by imputation."[8] He asserted that this is the basis of Paul's argument in Romans 5:

> For if by one man's offence death reigned by one; much more they which receive abundance of grace and of the gift of righteousness shall reign in life by one, Jesus Christ. Therefore, as by the offence of one judgment came upon all men to condemnation; even so by the righteousness of one the free gift came upon all men unto justification of life. For as by one man's disobedience many were made sinners, so by the obedience of one shall many be made righteous. (Romans 5:17-19)

Whitefield argued, on the basis of the parallelism of these verses, that just as Adam's guilt was imputed to the race, so Christ's righteousness is imputed to those whom God chooses for salvation.[9]

In the famous letter penned by Whitefield to John Wesley on the occasion of the latter's publication of his sermon "Free Grace," Whitefield questioned whether Wesley truly believed in original sin. Questioning Wesley's assertion that "thousands and millions of men, without any preceding offence or fault, were doomed to everlasting burnings," Whitefield queried:

> Do not they who believe God's dooming men to everlasting burnings, also believe, that God looked upon them as men fallen in Adam? And that the decree which ordained the punishment, first regarded the crime by which it was deserved? How then are they doomed without any preceding fault? Surely Mr. Wesley will own God's justice, in imputing Adam's sin to his posterity; and also, that after Adam fell, and his posterity in him, God might justly have passed them all by, without sending his own Son to be a saviour for any one. Unless you heartily agree to both these points, you do not believe original sin aright.[10]

Whitefield, while believing original sin "aright," and counting it as a doctrine necessary for a proper belief in the nature of God and salvation, did not count it as a doctrine necessary for an individual's acceptance by his "catholic spirit." For while Whitefield encouraged his hearers to have a right understanding of original sin, and while an awareness of one's sinfulness is a prerequisite to conversion, it was not a litmus test of fellowship. He might bluntly state in a sermon, "And if you have never felt the weight of original sin, do not call yourselves Christians,"[11] but deny by his relationships that this was a requirement for evangelical ecumenic-ity.[12]

Although accused of not believing in original sin "aright," Wesley did hold it as a foundational theological belief. In fact, the longest of his theological treatises is *The Doctrine of Original Sin*. While this was written a full fifteen years after the letter in which Whitefield questioned Wesley's orthodoxy on the issue, Wesley nonetheless had a highly developed view of humanity's fall and its consequences. This is illustrated on at least one occasion when Wesley refers to the doctrine of original sin as one of three "essentials" upon which clergy of kindred mind must agree.[13]

Wesley's estimate of human nature is as bleak as Whitefield's. In his sermon, "Original Sin," Wesley called original sin "that total loss of righteousness and true holiness which we sustained by the sin of our first parent."[14] He proclaimed, "Know your disease! . . . Ye were born in sin . . . . By nature ye are wholly cor-rupted . . . . In Adam ye all died."[15] Throughout the sermon, Wesley argued against the prevailing philosophy that stated while humans may be born with par-ticular "vices," at heart, all are born with a "natural good" that "much over-balances the evil."[16] Wesley contends that, far from having innate goodness, hu-mans are "conceived in sin" and "shapen in wickedness," possess a "carnal mind, which is enmity against God" that infects the soul to such a degree that all motives are "continually" evil.[17]

Wesley continues to paint the human condition in dark strokes in his sermon, "God's Love to Fallen Man:"

> It was by his (Adam's) wilful rebellion against God that "sin entered into the world." "By one man's disobedience," as the Apostle observes, "the many," . . . as many as were then in the loins of their forefather, "were made," or constituted, "sinners:" not only deprived of the favour of God, but also of his image; of all virtue, righteousness, and true holiness; and sunk partly into the image of the devil, in pride, malice, and all other dia-bolical tempers; partly into the image of the brute, being fallen under the dominion of brutal passions and grovelling appetites. Hence also death entered into the world, with all his forerunners and attendants, pain, sick-ness, and a whole train of uneasy as well as unholy passions and tem-pers.[18]

This sermon made its appearance in the *Arminian Magazine* in 1782, twelve years after Whitefield's death. Yet there is enough early evidence to indicate that Wesley had a highly developed and orthodox view of the fall and original sin. As early as 1730, Wesley preached, "Our business is to know in particular that we are all originally foolish and vicious, and that there is no truth in our whole religion more absolutely necessary to be known than this. Because if man be not naturally corrupt, then all religion. . . is vain, seeing it is all built on this — all method[s] of cure presupposing the disease."[19]

Whitefield and Wesley were equally in agreement when it came to the transmission of original sin through Adam's progeny. Whitefield had accused Wesley of "not believing in original sin aright" if he did not accept the fact that Adam's sin was imputed to the human race and that God had every right to withhold the offer of salvation from all he chose. Concerning the imputation of Adam's guilt, Wesley's theology paralleled that of Whitefield. Both viewed Adam as the "federal head" of humanity. Commenting on Romans 5:12, Wesley notes that in Adam, "all have sinned . . . . These words assign the reason why death came upon all men, infants themselves not excepted, for that all have sinned."[20] Kenneth Collins points out that here, Wesley is closely aligned with the standard Calvinistic belief in Adam as the federal head of humanity.[21] In the treatise *On Original Sin*, Wesley quotes a colorful description from Boston's "Fourfold State of Man," "Adam's sin corrupted man's nature, and leavened the whole lump of mankind. We putrefied in Adam as our root. The root was poisoned, and so the branches were envenomed . . . . We were in him representatively, as our moral head; we were in him seminally, as our natural head. Hence we fell in him."[22] But while, as Lindstrom contends, Wesley does believe that the new life offered by Christ "is paralleled by death through Adam," Wesley does not believe that the merits of Christ are imputed to humanity in the same way that Adam's sin is imputed.[23] It is here, in the doctrines that spring from their conception of original sin, that Wesley and Whitefield's theological differences are evident. The "righteousness" that is "imputed" to believers is not sanctifying grace. While Whitefield contends that even this grace is imputed, Wesley argues that sanctifying grace is imparted.[24] This will be addressed in detail when discussing their views on sanctification.

On the theological issue that is most basic to their respective theologies, Whitefield and Wesley differed but little. Both believed human nature to be corrupt due to the sinful nature inherited from Adam. As physical attributes are passed from one generation to another, this attribute of sin is also passed on to successive generations. Both would argue, as will be seen later, that original sin made the salvific work of Christ necessary. Each would contend that original sin makes God's grace so much more amazing and incomprehensible. Whitefield and Wesley "believed original sin aright." Indications of their differences can be seen in how they believed God's grace was activated in individual lives.

Whitefield and Wesley on Predestination

Original sin may have been a foundational theological belief for Whitefield and Wesley, but election is the tenet generally identified as Whitefield's hallmark.

Unconditional election held an integral position in the Calvinistic theology of Jonathan Edwards, Howell Harris, the Erskines, and their brother in faith, George Whitefield. "Free grace" for Whitefield meant that God freely and unconditionally bestowed his forgiveness on those he selected. This also meant that God could withhold his grace from whomever he pleased. "I freely acknowledge," wrote Whitefield to Wesley, "I believe the doctrine of reprobation, in this view, that God intends to give saving grace, through Jesus Christ, only to a certain number, and that the rest of mankind, after the fall of Adam, being justly left of God to continue in sin, will at last suffer that eternal death, which is its proper wages."[25] Whitefield defends his argument by asserting that election is not only a scriptural doctrine but also one that the Church of England gives credence to in its seventeenth Article of Religion. The Article that Whitefield defends and Wesley ignores states:

> Predestination to life is the everlasting purpose of God, whereby before the foundations of the world were laid, he hath constantly decreed by his counsel secret to us, to deliver from the curse and damnation those whom he hath chosen in Christ out of mankind, and to bring them by Christ to everlasting salvation, as vessels made to honour. Wherefore they which be indued with so excellent a benefit of God be called according to God's purpose by his Spirit, working in due season; they through grace obey the calling; they be justified freely; they be made sons of God by adoption; they be made like the image of his only begotten Son Jesus Christ; they walk religiously in good works and at length by God's mercy, they attain to everlasting felicity.[26]

The Article makes a strong statement concerning "predestination to eternal life," and an underlying, yet evident appeal for reprobation. The seventeenth Article declares that when the godly consider predestination, it brings them great joy, but when the doctrine is pondered by "curious and carnal persons, lacking the Spirit of Christ, (who) have continually before their eyes the sentence of God's predestination," it leads to "desperation or recklessness." For Whitefield to argue for "double predestination" from such ambiguous wording was a bit presumptuous. He also neglected, as Outler points out, that "the predestinarian interpretation of the Articles had in fact been declined by the majority of Anglican divines in the seven decades following the collapse of the Puritan Commonwealth."[27] Browne admits that the motivation behind the English Reformers' wording of the Article remains somewhat of a mystery; it "is truly a question of considerable difficulty."[28] As for Wesley's decision not to bring Article XVII into the discussion, the reason behind it is no doubt his belief that the general tenor of the Articles included a belief in the availability of universal redemption. While not including Article XVII in his 1784 compilation (there were thirteen other Articles he chose not to use as well), he did include other Articles that speak of the unlimited nature of the atonement. Article II, defended by Anglican and Methodist alike, notes that

Christ died "to reconcile his Father to us and to be a sacrifice not only for original guilt but also for all actual sins of men."[29] Article VII declares that "everlasting life is offered to mankind by Christ," with Articles XV and XXXI providing further support.[30] The commentators on the Articles also point to the "disclaimer" provided in the last paragraph of Article XVII as "proof" that double predestination was not the intent of the framers. "Furthermore we must receive God's promises in such wise as they be generally set forth to us in Holy Scripture; and in our doings that the will of God is to be followed which we have, expressly declared to us in the Word of God."[31] Bicknell argues that while a Calvinistic interpretation may be possible by looking only at the beginning of the Article, the closing sentences do not leave that option open. He interprets "generally" to mean "universally, for all men."[32] Wesley undoubtedly came to the same conclusion.

Whifield's scriptural defense of the doctrine of election is apparent in his response to Wesley's sermon, "Free Grace." He questions how Wesley could have the audacity to preach a sermon on unlimited atonement from a text Whitefield maintained was a clear expression of election. Wesley had chosen for a text Romans 8:32, "He that spared not his own Son, but delivered him up for us all, how shall he not with him also freely give us all things?" The exegetical difference hinged on the interpretation of the word "all." For whom was Christ "delivered up?" While Wesley would maintain that Christ was "delivered up" for all people who would respond to him in faith, Whitefield understood "all" to mean "the elect." Believing that Paul wrote in Romans 8 of "the privileges of those only who are really in Christ," Whitefield argues that the word "all" refers to "only those that are in Christ."[33] As with most of the disagreements between Wesley and Whitefield, language played an important role in the election debate. Language was far from meaningless to these leaders of British Methodism. Their arguments fell on each other's deaf ears due in large part to their individual definition of terms. While they both may have been using the same words, one wonders if they truly understood the direction from which the other was addressing the issue. And if they did understand, were they willing to listen to each other's definitions? Wesley did believe in election, in fact, in his tract *Predestination Calmly Considered*, he offers what he believes to be the two scriptural definitions of election. First, election can be an "absolute and unconditional" appointment from God for certain individuals to perform a particular mission. Wesley notes that this "election" can be of a believer or an unbeliever, and has nothing to do with one's eternal salvation. Secondly, biblical election for Wesley means "a divine appointment of some men to eternal happiness," but this form of election is completely conditional. Wesley holds that "all true believers" are rightly called by the Scriptures "elect."[34] In other words, all who receive Christ by faith become the "elect," for God has decreed to save all who will believe. This decree means "God will not change and man cannot resist."[35] Wesley painstakingly endeavors to define what he means by election. This tract was written a full ten years after the initial rift with Whitefield, and while their personal relationship remained cordial, the camp they represented were past listening to reasoned definitions from either side. Nevertheless, their personal relationship weathered the storm of controversy that was fueled by the rhetoric of their followers. Here, too, Whitefield's popularity as a preacher may well have contributed to his success in spreading the Calvinist doctrine of unconditional election and reprobation. Many would gladly listen to the "Grand Itinerant" who would not wade through Wesley's tract on predestination! Key to this contentious issue was the question over the roles of God and humanity in the salvation process. According to Whitefield, humanity's fall was so complete, that the race is utterly incapable of saving itself. He wrote to a clergyman:

> I hope we shall catch fire from each other, and that there will be an holy emulation amongst us, who shall most debase man and exalt the Lord Jesus. Nothing but the doctrines of the Reformation can do this. All others leave freewill in man, and make him, in part at least, a Saviour to himself. My soul come not near the secret of those who teach such things, mine honour be not thou united to them. I know Christ is all in all. Man is nothing: he hath a free will to go to hell, but none to go to heaven, till God worketh in him to will and to do after his good pleasure. It is God must prevent, God must accompany, God must follow with his grace, or Jesus Christ will bleed in vain.[36]

For Whitefield, God's divine election to salvation was a necessary first step in the process of human redemption. Without God declaring the election of certain individuals for salvation, all humanity would be lost. God's election is based solely on his sovereignty, not on any meritorious works God in his foreknowledge might foresee. Here would appear to be a major theological difference: Whitefield believing that God elects with no human input; Wesley believing Christ died for all and "whosoever will" may accept the free gift of salvation. But upon further study, it is clear that the difference is one of theological language and emphasis. Little in the aforementioned letter that Whitefield wrote would have offended Wesley's convictions. Had Wesley read Whitefield's words, "It is God must prevent, God must accompany, God must follow with his grace, or Jesus Christ will bleed in vain," he would have been in full agreement. Along with Whitefield, Wesley believed that God was the author, initiator, means, and director of the entire redemption process. Whitefield may speak of God electing individuals to salvation before the foundation of the world, but Wesley would insist that God bestowed prevenient grace on all humanity, giving all the opportunity to become one of the elect. "Prevenient grace is the grace that begins to enable one to choose further to cooperate with saving grace."[37] Oden continues by noting that Wesley is in full agreement with the Church of England, whose Article on free will notes that "we have no power to do good works pleasant and acceptable to God, without the grace of God by Christ preventing us, that we may have a good will, and working with us, when we have that good will."[38] Wesley affirmed that it is impossible for humans, in and of themselves, to make the "first move" in their relationship with God. But God has already done that by providing the grace necessary for people to respond to him in faith. "Salvation begins," said Wesley, "with what is usually termed (and very properly) preventing grace; including the first wish to please God, the first dawn of light concerning his will, and the first slight transient conviction of having sinned against him."[39] According to Wesley, prevenient grace prepared the person stained by original sin and their own corruption to receive subsequent stages of grace. The next stages of grace, however, are resistible. Prevenient grace only makes a person's "first steps toward saving faith" possible.[40]

The sovereignty of God was another point both protagonists defended, while placing greater or lesser weight upon it. For Whitefield, denying the doctrine of unconditional election was denying God his sovereign right to choose certain ones for salvation and "pass by" those he chose as well. Whitefield vindicated God's absolute right to elect those whom he would for salvation. His doctrine can be summed up in words he wrote, "Jesus lives and reigns."[41] Wesley accuses the predestinarians of stressing the doctrine so vehemently as to exclude God's other attributes. He implies that the Calvinists view "God's sovereign power as the ground of unconditional reprobation," then accuses them of raising God's sovereignty to the position of the most important of his attributes: "For the Scripture nowhere speaks of this single attribute as separate from the rest. Much less does it anywhere speak of the sovereignty of God as singly disposing the eternal states of men."[42] Instead of God's sovereignty superceding all other attributes, Wesley argues that "God proceeds according to the known rules of his justice and mercy, but never assigns his sovereignty as the cause why any man is punished with everlasting destruction . . . . The sovereignty of God is then never to be brought to supersede his justice."[43] Wesley contends that "unconditional reprobation" is completely incompatible with right belief in God's justice. Wesley's belief in the sovereignty of God, while of different emphasis than Whitefield's, is no less lofty. He asserts that God's sovereignty is exhibited in the decree that "He that believeth shall be saved: he that believeth not shall be damned." It is seen in the decisions involved with the general creation, in giving "natural endowments" and spiritual gifts to humanity, in the circumstances surrounding one's birth, and the "ordering" of one's health, employment, and friendships. "But," he continues, "in disposing the eternal states of men, it is clear that not sovereignty alone, but justice, mercy, and truth hold the reins."[44] Wesley concludes:

> To tear up the very roots of reprobation, and of all doctrines that have a necessary connexion therewith, God declares in his Word these three things, and that explicitly, in so many terms: 1. "Christ died for all," namely, all that "were dead" in sin, as the words immediately following fix the sense. Here is the fact affirmed. 2. "He is the propitiation for the sins of the whole world, even of all those for whom he died. Here is the

consequence of his dying for all. And, 3. "He died for all, that they should not live unto themselves, but unto him which died for them," that they might be saved from their sins. Here is the design, the end, of his dying for them. Now show me the Scriptures wherein God declares in equally express terms (1) Christ did not die for all, but for some only; (2) Christ is not "the propitiation for the sins of the whole world," And (3) he did not die for all, at least, not with the intent "that they should live unto him who died for them."[45]

Whitefield and Wesley employed a common theological language, but the meaning behind the language differed in their definitions of original sin, election, and God's sovereignty. Both defended original sin. Both defended election and God's sovereignty as cherished biblical doctrines. For both, original sin plunged humanity into depths of spiritual darkness from which no one was able to free themselves. God, in implementing his sovereign will, decreed the salvation of the elect. Already it is evident that the theological differences between Wesley and Whitefield were not based on orthodox versus unorthodox beliefs. The differences were based much more on emphasis: Whitefield emphasizing humanity's complete inability to do anything about its sinful situation; Wesley emphasizing that God had gifted humanity with the means of cooperating with God in the salvific process. Wesley guarded against taking anything away from God's initiating the redemptive process through his doctrine of prevenient grace. God was still in control; he simply graced humanity with the ability to respond to his divine invitation to salvation. Randy Maddox has aptly referred to this as "responsible grace."[46]

Whitefield and Wesley on Justification by Faith

The Protestant Reformation did not remain a Continental movement for long. Within decades after Luther's posting of the Ninety-Five Theses, the principles that he held dear had spread to the British Isles. Only two centuries later, the major premises of the Reformation, "Scripture alone," "Grace alone," and "Faith alone," were experiencing their own "renaissance" as integral parts of the English revivals. Whitefield and Wesley agreed upon all three of these major themes, understanding them to be vital to genuine Christianity.

Justification, for Whitefield, was a juridical term meaning that the one so standing had been "acquitted, and looked upon as righteous in the sight of God."[47] Whitefield proclaims:

(Justification is) as though . . . you have your sins forgiven and are looked upon by God as though you never had offended him at all: for that is the meaning of the word justified, in almost all the passages of holy scripture where this word is mentioned. . . . For it is a law-term, and alludes to a judge acquitting an accused criminal of the thing laid to his charge.[48]

God justifies in response to the believer's faith. However, lest believers become proud, believing that "their" faith has saved them, Whitefield reminded his hearer that even the faith to believe is a gift of God: "When a sinner is enabled to lay hold on Christ's righteousness by faith, he is freely justified from all his sins."[49] An individual may confess to belief in God, but Whitefield says this cannot be the case "until God has put his faith in us; then we have in our souls a new life in Christ."[50] The elect, proclaims Whitefield, must be "enabled" by God to be justified.[51]

Further, the elect are not justified due to any foreseen merit of their own. They are justified solely because Christ's righteousness is imputed to them:

> By having Christ's righteousness imputed to them, they are dead to the law, as a covenant of works; Christ has fulfilled it for them, and in their stead. Does death threaten them? They need not fear: the sting of death is sin, the strength of sin is the law; but God has given them the victory by imputing to them the righteousness of the Lord Jesus.[52]

Having Christ's righteousness credited to the believer's account is essential, for the sinner stands spiritually bankrupt before a holy God. It is only through Christ's righteousness that one can be justified. "This righteousness must be imputed, or counted over to us, and applied by faith to our hearts, or else we can in no wise be justified in God's sight."[53] Whitefield further stressed the importance, not only of the imputation of the merits of Christ's death, but also the imputation of the perfect obedience of his life. "Both these jointly," says Whitefield, "make up that complete righteousness which is to be imputed to us, as the disobedience of our first parents was made ours by imputation."[54] It is vain for people to talk about being converted until they "are clothed in his glorious imputed righteousness: the consequence of this imputation, or application of a Mediator's righteousness to the soul, will be a conversion from sin to holiness."[55]

Wesley stood by Whitefield as a fellow defender of the doctrine of justification by faith. In his sermon on this theme, Wesley replays the history of God's plan of redemption, reminding his audience that humanity, created in the image of God, fell into sin and stood in need of a Savior. God, in his mercy, sent his Son to be "a second general Parent and Representative of the whole human race." By offering himself as a sinless sacrifice for the sins of the world, he made satisfaction for sinful humanity:

This, therefore, is the general ground of the whole doctrine of justification. By the sin of the first Adam, who was not only the father, but likewise the representative, of us all, we all fell short of the favour of God; we all became children of wrath; or, as the Apostle expresses it, "judgment came upon all men to condemnation." Even so, by the sacrifice for sin made by the Second Adam, as the Representative of us all, God is so far reconciled to all the world, that he hath given them a new covenant; the plain condition whereof being once fulfilled, "there is no more condemnation" for us, but "we are justified freely by his grace, through the redemption that is in Jesus Christ."[56]

Thus, "the plain scriptural notion of justification is pardon, the forgiveness of sins."[57] Wesley expands on this in his *Principles of a Methodist*, written in 1742:

I believe three things must go together in our justification: Upon God's part, his great mercy and grace; upon Christ's part, the satisfaction of God's justice, by . . . offering his body, and shedding his blood; and upon our part, true and living faith in the merits of Jesus Christ. So that in our justification there is not only God's mercy and grace, but his justice also. And so the grace of God does not shut out the righteousness of God in our justification; but only shuts out the righteousness of man, that is, the righteousness of our works.[58]

Justification, then, is dependent on God's grace, Christ's sacrifice, and human faith. The faith that leads to justification is more than mere mental assent to basic Christian dogma, although Wesley did not discount intellectual faith as part of the picture. To be justifying faith, it must also include "a hearty trust in the person and work of Christ; and on a sensate or experiential level, it embraces a trust that is nothing less than . . . a 'divine evidence and conviction' that Christ 'loved me, and gave himself for me.'"[59] Again, we find Wesley and Whitefield in agreement on their belief that the witness of the Holy Spirit is central to the believer's comfort and assurance. In one of his rare appeals to the Articles of Religion of the Church of England, Whitefield contends, "the godly consideration of predestination, and election in Christ, is full of sweet, pleasant, unspeakable comfort to godly persons, and such as feel in themselves the working of the Spirit of Christ, mortifying the works of the flesh, and their earthly members, and drawing their minds to high and heavenly things, as well because it does greatly establish and confirm their faith of eternal salvation."[60]

The casual student of Wesley may be surprised to learn that Wesley was in agreement with Whitefield, even on the point of the imputed righteousness of Christ, at least in the stage of justification. While admitting that he did not find the phrase "imputed righteousness" in the Scriptures, he did believe that the meaning is present. Wesley quoted Philippians 3:8, 9; "That I may win Christ, and be found in him, not having my own righteousness." He reminded his reader of 1 Corinthians 1:30; "Jesus Christ is made of God unto us wisdom, and righteousness, and sanctification, and redemption." He mentioned Abraham, who, "believed in the Lord, and (God) counted it to him for righteousness" (Genesis 15:6). These all bore witness to the fact that when a penitent sinner is justified, the merits of Christ are credited to that individual.[61] But while Whitefield argued for the imputation of Christ's obedient life as the basis of the believer's sanctification, Wesley could not extend his belief that far. Wesley wanted to guard against the dangers of antinomianism. As Oden describes it, "we should never talk an easy game of imputation without taking seriously the process of behavioral sanctification."[62] But as far as justification by faith was concerned, Wesley and Whitefield differed "but a hair's breadth." On this key doctrine of the Reformation, there was consensus among the two leading figures of the English Revival. It would continue to be a unifying principle.

Whitefield and Wesley on the New Birth

Few would argue that on the issue of the New Birth, Whitefield and Wesley were kindred spirits. Timothy Smith notes that all evangelicals of the period, be they Methodist, Anglican, Congregationalist, or Pietist, "all stressed the work of the Holy Spirit in bringing sinners to repentance and faith in Christ, assuring them of forgiveness, and, by His presence thereafter in their hearts, nurturing in them the love and holiness that please God."[63] Indeed, the battle cry of the Evangelical Revival in England was, "Ye must be born again."

Of all the similarities between Whitefield and Wesley — both educated at Oxford, both ordained by the Church of England, both committed to Scriptural Christianity, and both dedicated to the spread of the gospel, this common devotion to the doctrine of regeneration bound them together. Along with their common belief in justification by faith, this common belief did as much as anything to bring them back together after their split. Whitefield, the junior member of the duo, experienced the New Birth three years prior to Wesley. He writes of his conversion experience, that was due in part to the influence of Charles Wesley:

> In a short time he (Charles) let me have another book, entitled, *The Life of God in the Soul of Man*; (and, though I had fasted, watched and prayed, and received the Sacrament so long, yet I never knew what true religion was, till God sent me that excellent treatise by the hands of my never-to-be-forgotten friend.)
>
> At my first reading it, I wondered what the author meant by saying, "That some falsely placed religion in going to church, doing hurt to no one, being constant in the duties of the closet, and now and then reaching out their hands to give alms to their poor neighbors." "Alas!"

thought I, "if this be not true religion, what is?" God soon showed me; for in reading a few lines further, that "true religion was union of the soul with God, and Christ formed within us," a ray of Divine light was instantaneously darted in upon my soul, and from that moment, but not till then, did I know that I must be a new creature.[64]

Within two years, Whitefield completed his studies at Oxford, received his Holy Orders, and began preaching the necessity of the New Birth.

Early in 1737, Whitefield first preached his sermon "On the Nature and Necessity of our Regeneration or New Birth in Jesus Christ, which he was "prevailed upon" to print in August of the same year. According to Whitefield, the sermon was the means by which God "began the awakening at London, Bristol, Gloucester, and Gloucestershire."[65] Taking as his text 2 Corinthians 5:17, "If any man be in Christ, he is a new creature," Whitefield develops his theology of regeneration by describing what it means to be "in Christ." It is much more than just outward profession:

To be in Him not only by an outward profession, but by an inward change and purity of heart, and cohabitation of His Holy Spirit. To be in Him, so as to be mystically united to Him by a true and lively faith, and thereby to receive spiritual virtue from Him, as the members of the natural body do from the head, or the branches from the vine.[66]

Becoming a new creature in Christ means "being altered as to the qualities and tempers of our minds, that we must entirely forget what manner of persons we once were."[67] Whitefield sees the doctrine of regeneration "writ large" on every page of Holy Scripture, informing his hearers that when the biblical authors speak of being "born again," of "putting off the old man," and "putting on the new," of being "renewed in the spirit of our minds," and becoming "new creatures," they were all indicative of the fact that "Christianity requires a thorough, real, inward change of heart."[68]

The whole of Whitefield's preaching portfolio is filled with reminders to his hearers that regeneration is a necessary component of the Christian life. In his sermon "The Method of Grace," he admonishes his audience:

. . . the promise of rest is made to them only upon their coming and believing, and taking him to be their God and their all. Before we can ever have peace with God, we must be justified by faith through our Lord Jesus Christ, we must be enabled to apply Christ to our hearts, we must have Christ brought home to our souls. . . . My dear friends, were you ever married to Jesus Christ? Did you ever close with Christ by a lively faith, so as to feel Christ in your heart, so as to hear him speaking peace to your souls?[69]

And in "Christ, the Believer's Wisdom, Righteousness, Sanctification and Redemption" he proclaims:

And O what a privilege is this! to be changed from beasts into saints, and from a devilish, to be made partakers of a divine nature; to be translated from the kingdom of Satan, into the kingdom of God's dear Son! to put off the old man which is corrupt, and to put on the new man, which is created after God, in righteousness and true holiness! O what an unspeakable blessing is this! I almost stand amazed at the contemplation thereof.[70]

References to the "changed nature" abound:

(The one who is justified) shall have peace with God — a peace which passeth all understanding; not only peace, but joy in believing; he shall be translated from the kingdom of Satan, to the kingdom of God's dear Son: he shall dwell in Christ, and Christ in him: he shall be one with Christ, and Christ one with him . . . he shall be filled with all the fullness of God.[71]

Hast thou the thing promised? The thing promised is, all peace, and all joy — the thing promised is a new heart — the thing promised is a new nature; and therefore David goes to God for the thing promised, and says, "Create in me a clean heart, O God, and renew a right spirit within me." Now is this the case of thy heart? The devil can never make a new creature. I am sure nothing but an almighty power can take away the heart of stone, and give a heart of flesh. Has God wrought this in thee?[72]

Clearly, for Whitefield, the New Birth was a foundational doctrine of the Christian faith. Inseparable from regeneration are the doctrines of justification by faith, holiness, and the witness of the Holy Spirit. Whitefield, the Grand Itinerant, is elucidating basic evangelical doctrine with which Wesley would be in complete agreement, and outlining a basis for evangelical ecumenicity.

Elsewhere, Whitefield writes of an encounter he and John Wesley had with two Anglican clergymen and "some other strong opposers of the doctrine of the New Birth." Of their meeting, Whitefield writes, "Now, therefore, I am convinced there is a fundamental difference between us and them. They believe only an outward Christ, we further believe that He must be inwardly formed in our hearts also."[73] For Whitefield, the New Birth was dramatic, not static. It was experiential. It would be evidenced in the believer's life. Just as natural birth is accompanied by intense sensation, so the New Birth must be experienced intensely. The doctrine was important; the feeling at least equally so.[74]

Wesley was no stranger to the doctrine of regeneration. He agreed with Whitefield that "an unapplied Christ is no Christ at all." Hence, regardless of one's interpretation of the event, his Aldersgate experience, where he "felt his heart strangely warmed," believing that Christ had indeed died for his sins, stands as a defining moment in his life in which belief and experience were joined together.

Using the language of the Scriptures, Wesley indicates that regeneration is being "born of the Spirit." It includes "a sure trust and confidence in God, that, through the merits of Christ, (the believer's) sins are forgiven, and he reconciled to the favour of God."[75] He outlines the evidence of the new birth in a believer's life:

> . . . to be a child of God: It is so to believe in God, through Christ, as "not to commit sin," and to enjoy at all times, and in all places, that "peace of God which passeth all understanding." It is, so to hope in God through the Son of his love, as to have not only the "testimony of a good conscience," but also the Spirit of God "bearing witness with your spirits, that ye are the children of God;" . . . . It is, so to love God, who hath thus loved you, as you never did any creature: So that ye are constrained to love all men as yourselves; with a love not only ever burning in your hearts, but flaming out in all your actions and conversations, and making your whole life one "labour of love" . . .[76]

Wesley's belief in the experiential nature of the New Birth is no less evident than Whitefield's. In his sermon, "The New Birth," Wesley affirms that the unregenerate has "spiritual senses" that are "all locked up." But when the person experiences the new birth, "there is a total change in all these particulars." Spiritual "eyes" are opened to see "the light of the glory of God." Spiritual "ears" are unstopped to hear "the inward voice of God" declaring sins forgiven.

> He "feels in his heart" to use the language of our Church, "the mighty working of the Spirit of God;" . . . He feels, is inwardly sensible of, the graces which the Spirit of God works in his heart. He feels, he is conscious of, a "peace which passeth all understanding." He many times feels such a joy in God as is "unspeakable and full of glory." He feels "the love of God shed abroad in his heart by the Holy Ghost which is given unto him;" and all his spiritual senses are then exercised to discern spiritual good and evil.[77]

Regeneration for Wesley was:

. . . that great change which God works in the soul when he brings it into life; when he raises it from the death of sin to the life of righteousness. It is the change wrought in the whole soul by the almighty Spirit of God when it is "created anew in Christ Jesus;" when it is "renewed after the image of God, in righteousness and true holiness;" when the love of the world is changed into the love of God; pride into humility; passion into meekness; hatred, envy, malice, into a sincere, tender, disinterested love for all mankind. In a word, it is that change whereby the earthly, sensual, devilish mind is turned into the "mind which was in Christ Jesus."[78]

Wesley contended that the New Birth is the "gateway" to sanctification, and that just as natural birth entails a change from one state to another, so the New Birth "implies as great a change in the soul." It was not simply a change in behavior, but an inward change from "unholy" to "holy" tempers.[79] It was a change, "from spiritual death to spiritual life."[80] Regeneration involved "an entire change of heart."[81] And in responding to a work titled, "A Caution against Religious Delusion," Wesley wrote:

(The New Birth) must infer not only an outward change . . . but a thorough change of heart, an inward renewal in the spirit of our mind. Accordingly, "the old man" implies infinitely more than outward evil conversation, even "an evil heart of unbelief," corrupted by pride and a thousand deceitful lusts. Of consequence, the "new man" must imply infinitely more than outward good conversation, even "a good heart, which after God is created in righteousness and true holiness;" a heart full of that faith which, working by love, produces all holiness of conversation.[82]

Whitefield and Wesley, along with other evangelicals of the era, agreed on the necessity of the New Birth. Regeneration as such was not a point of contention between the two. Consensus had effectively been achieved. The only difference appears in the related discussion of the mode of operation of salvation. "For Wesley grace is operative positively on all men; for Whitefield it is applied redemptively only to the eternally elect in Christ. For Wesley the eternal decree of God in Christ is to set blessing and cursing before men whom He has already graciously enabled to choose."[83]

Whitefield and Wesley on Sanctification

We have documented that Whitefield viewed sanctification as just another benefit of the imputed righteousness of Christ in the believer's life. Unlike the "alleged antinomians" that Wesley believes will be created by a Whitefieldian interpretation of sanctification, Whitefield holds sanctification in high esteem. He clearly affirms that sanctification is much more than "bare outward reformation," "a few transient convictions, or a little legal sorrow." Sanctification is "a total renovation of the whole man: by the righteousness of Christ." Through it, "believers come legally . . . they are made spiritually, alive; by the one they are entitled to, by the other they are made meet for, glory. They are sanctified, therefore, throughout, in spirit, soul, and body."[84] Preaching from Jeremiah 23:5-6 on "The Lord our Righteousness," Whitefield queries:

> Is Christ your sanctification, as well as your outward righteousness? For the word righteousness, in the text, not only implies Christ's personal righteousness imputed to us, but also holiness wrought in us. These two, God has joined together. He never did, he never does, he never will, put them asunder. If you are justified by the blood, you are also sanctified by the Spirit, of our Lord.[85]

Whitefield endeavors to separate himself from the Arminians, whom he accuses of making sanctification the cause instead of the effect of justification: "For Christ's righteousness, or that which Christ has done in our stead without us, is the sole cause of our acceptance in the sight of God (justification), and of all holiness wrought in us . . . our sanctification at best, in this life, is not complete: though we be delivered from the power, we are not freed from the in-being of sin."[86]

Whitefield also parries the Arminian accusation that a belief in imputed righteousness will lead to antinomianism by reminding his hearers that good works, holy living, will be evidenced in the life of the believer who has been truly sanctified. They will flow from the individual believer out of a thankful spirit and an obedient heart. While maintaining that in the Sermon on the Mount, Jesus was lobbying for "inward piety, such as poverty of spirit, meekness, holy mourning, purity of heart, especially hungering and thirsting after righteousness," Whitefield declares that Jesus "recommends good works, as an evidence of our having his righteousness imputed to us."[87] In his sermon "Repentance and Conversion," he thunders:

> . . . how can (the Calvinists) be charged with being enemies to Sanctification, who so strenuously insists on its being the genuine fruit, and unquestionable proof of the imputation of the righteousness of Christ, and application of it by the Spirit of grace? They that are truly converted to Jesus, and are justified by faith in the Son of God, will take care to evidence their conversion, not only by having grace implanted in their hearts, but by that grace diffusing itself through every faculty of the soul, and making an universal change in the whole man.[88]

Holy living was not optional; God expected it.

John Wesley's name is most often associated with the doctrine of Christian perfection, so much so that one may be led to believe that he was the originator of the doctrine. Indeed, he called the doctrine "the grand depositum" of the Methodists. Yet from his indebtedness to Taylor, á Kempis, Law, and all of Christian antiquity, including the Scriptures, it is invalid to say that Wesley had discovered something new. He simply gave new and popular expression to a generally forgotten doctrine.

In its simplest expression, Wesley calls Christian perfection "loving God with all our heart, and mind, and soul."[89] Few on either the Calvinist or Arminian side would have had a problem affirming this. But when asked if this means that all "inward sin is taken away," Wesley replied, "Undoubtedly; or how can we be said to be 'saved from all our uncleannesses?'"[90] Further, "The loving God with all our heart, mind, soul, and strength . . . implies, that no wrong temper, none contrary to love, remains in the soul; and that all the thoughts, words, and actions, are governed by pure love."[91] This is where the rub with Whitefield entered the scene. Whitefield could not accept the fact that the "in-being" of sin could be taken away short of the saint entering heaven. When one was justified, Whitefield believed that the power of sin was broken. But to believe that sin could be totally uprooted, was, to him, pure audacity.

Wesley counters objections that many had to this doctrine. Upon hearing or reading about Christian perfection, some concluded that Wesley was proposing that one could be freed of all human frailties. This was not the case. As long as one is a pilgrim on this earth, each will be subject to errors in judgment and mistakes common to all humanity. While these cannot justly be termed "sin," Wesley says that as God is pure holiness, even these mistakes, if not covered by the atoning blood of Christ, would be sufficient to separate the individual from Christ for all eternity.[92] Also troublesome to many was Wesley's belief that sanctification required a "second work of grace" beyond the regenerative work. "It is not so early as justification," he wrote, but "not so late as death."[93] This immediately put him at odds with Whitefield, who believed that one is regenerated and sanctified at one moment, and not freed from the "in-being" of sin until death. Wesley did not believe, however, that this was merely a crisis event. Professors to perfection may be able to point to a "time and place" much like a born-again believer could, but Wesley was adamant that spiritual maturation took place both prior to and after the sanctifying event. Those justified are admonished in Scripture to "go on to perfection," and Wesley added his encouragement, "It is constantly both preceded and followed by a gradual work."[94] Earlier he penned, "I believe this perfection is always wrought in the soul by a simple act of faith; consequently, in an instant. But I believe a gradual work, both preceding and following that instant."[95]

Justification may be "initial sanctification," Wesley would say, but there are distinctions between justification and sanctification. Oden condenses the differentiation:

> Justification is the work of the Son, sanctification of the Spirit. They are integrally connected since God is one, and inseparable because "the Lord . . . is the Spirit" (2 Corinthians 3:17), yet distinguishable because the mission of the Spirit is to bring to full expression the ministry of the Son.[96]

For Wesley, justification is "what God does for us through his Son;" sanctification is "what he works in us by his Spirit."[97] Contra Whitefield, Wesley believed that "faith would result in a real change in the believer where, by the grace of God, Christ's righteousness would be imparted to the person, who would not only be accounted righteous but would become righteous (sanctified or holy)."[98] But far from depending upon human effort for holy living, "the teaching of perfecting grace is not finally about the power of human freedom, but the power of grace totally to transform freedom. This transformation is best understood as Christ's own forming in us, and secondarily as our yielding ourselves to be formed by Christ."[99]

While it appears that Whitefield and Wesley were at least as deeply divided over the issue of sanctification as they were over predestination, toward the end of Whitefield's life, the two may have been engaged in seeking common ground even on this divisive issue. Both protagonists attacked William Warbuton's work that denigrated the work of the Holy Spirit. According to Timothy Smith, "Both stressed the scriptural promise that the gift of the Holy Spirit in the new birth would empower believers to live a righteous life."[100] He further indicated that in Whitefield's response to Warburton, he employs phraseology that Wesley used to speak of both initial and entire sanctification. "Divine tempers," says Whitefield, "are flowers not to be gathered in nature's garden. They are exotics; planted originally in heaven, and in the great work of the new birth transplanted by the Holy Ghost, not only into the hearts of the first apostles or primitive Christians but into the hearts of all true believers, even to the end of the world."[101] Interestingly enough, the sermons from which the terminology comes were originally preached from 1739 to 1741, during the time of the most visible separation between Whitefield and Wesley.[102]

In a response to Smith's original article "George Whitefield and Wesleyan Perfectionism," Leon O. Hynson agrees that there were obvious points of agreement between Whitefield and Wesley even on the "issues directly relating to sanctification." Both agreed on the following points:

> 1. No sinless perfection is possible in this life (*non posse non peccare*).

2. The norm and expectation for the Christian life is holy, not sinful, living.

3. This means subjective, personal holiness in the life of the regenerate.

4. The dominion of sin is broken in the regenerate by the power of the sanctifying Spirit.

5. The regenerate may avoid willful sin (*posse non peccare*).

6. Both hold an ontological or substantialist definition of original sin. They agree with the Church of England that the "corruption of sin remains in the regenerate." (Article 9)[103]

This is not to say they were in total agreement on the issue. Whitefield remained convinced of his belief that one is not delivered from the "in-being" of sin in this life. But he does move back toward an earlier belief in "subjective holiness" and Wesley moves toward the goal of "holiness of intention."[104] But Whitefield died before they got any closer. They were closer to consensus than many would care to admit.

Whitefield and Wesley on the Perseverance of the Saints

On this matter, to say that Whitefield believed it and Wesley did not, may sound simplistic, but comes very close to the truth. That being said, both men did believe that their "system" provided the best means for believers to be assured of the eternal grace of God and the security of one's faith. Both based that security in the integrity of the promises of God.

Whitefield simply followed the inherent logic of predestinarian theology. If God, in his sovereign mercy, elects certain individuals to salvation, then they will surely see ultimate salvation in heaven. For God to "elect" and then not "keep" would have been a logical error that Whitefield, to his credit, avoided. He comments on the Scripture "But of him are ye in Christ Jesus, who of God is made unto us wisdom, and righteousness, and sanctification, and redemption:"

This is a golden chain indeed! and, what is best of all, not one link can ever be broken asunder from another. Was there no other text in the book of God, this single one sufficiently proves the final perseverance of true believers: for never did God yet justify a man, whom he did not sanctify; nor sanctify one, whom he did not completely redeem and glorify: no! as for God, his way, his work, is perfect; he always carried on and finished the work he begun . . . . Those whom God has justified, he has in effect glorified: for as a man's worthiness was not the cause of God's giving him Christ's righteousness; so neither shall his unwor-

thiness be a cause of his taking it away; God's gifts and callings are
without repentance: and I cannot think they are clear in the notion of
Christ's righteousness, who deny the final perseverance of the saints.[105]

Writing to a "Mr. A" from Boston, Whitefield accuses believers in "sinless perfection" of being inconsistent. It is folly to believe that an individual may be
"perfect" in this life, yet still not be assured of eternal bliss. "What an absurdity
is this?"[106] What Whitefield forgot, or was unaware of, was that Wesley believed that perfection was a state from which one could fall. Thus entire sanctification was not assurance that an individual was eternally secure. Whitefield continues:

I hear many amongst you who begun in the spirit, are now ending in the
flesh. Christ hath freely justified them, i.e. entitled them to all his merits, and yet they must do so and so to keep themselves in a justified
state. Alas, this is sorry divinity; I have not so learned Christ. No, his
gifts and callings are without repentance. Whom he loves, he loves to
the end. Work I will, but not to keep myself in a justified state. My
Lord hath secured that; but I will work to shew my gratitude for his
putting me into a justified state.[107]

Within a few days, he wrote again:

. . . "Those whom (Christ) justified, them he also glorified;" so that if a
man was once justified, he remains so to all eternity. Here lies the an-
chor of all my hopes. Our Lord having once loved me, he will love me
to the end. This fills me with joy unspeakable and full of glory. I now
walk by faith. I work not to keep myself in a justified state . . .[108]

At the height of the separation between himself and Wesley, Whitefield, in
responding to Wesley's sermon "Free Grace," calls into question his reasoning
on there being no final perseverance. Wesley has noted that the predestinarian
view "tends to destroy the comforts of religion." Whitefield wonders how
Wesley can say such a thing. Just the opposite is the case! The fact that one can
know they are one of the elect and be assured that nothing "in all creation" can
take away their new life, is the greatest comfort that can be afforded. "This doctrine is my daily support," writes Whitefield. "I should utterly sink under a dread
of my impending trials, was I not firmly persuaded that God has chosen me in
Christ from before the foundation of the world, and that now being effectually
called, he will suffer none to pluck me out of his almighty hand."[109] Whitefield
wondered how anyone could live from day to day without the assurance his or

her soul was secure beyond reach. "Without the belief of the doctrine of election, and the immutability of the free love of God, I cannot see how it is possible
that any should have a comfortable assurance of eternal salvation."[110] He questions the kind of assurance Wesley offers — a person awakened to their sinful
state receives forgiveness from God, only to have to wonder whether they will
lose it in the future. What Whitefield believes God offers is the unquestionable
assurance that no adversary nor any failure on the believer's part is capable of
finally separating the Christian from the love of Christ. "That many have an
assurance they are in Christ today, but take no thought for, or are not assured
they shall be in him tomorrow, nay to all eternity, is rather their imperfection
and unhappiness, than their privilege."[111]

Wesley's view was not designed to leave believers in a state of uncertainty.
But neither was it intended to provide false hopes to those who wanted the benefits of regeneration but desired to continue a sinful lifestyle. In his *Minutes of
Some Late Conversations*, the question is asked, "Are works necessary to the
continuance of faith?" with the answer, "Without doubt; for a man may forfeit
the free gift of God, either by sins of omission or commission." But "can faith
be lost but for want of works?" "It cannot but through disobedience."[112] In other
words, losing one's salvation was not something that occurred accidentally, one
had to will it, want it, and "work" at it.

He further declares his beliefs in *Serious Thoughts upon the Perseverance
of the Saints*. The thesis he sets out to prove is, "I believe a saint may fall away;
that one who is holy or righteous in the judgment of God himself may nevertheless so fall from God as to perish everlastingly." He proceeds to enumerate the
biblical texts he believes prove that apostasy is possible.[113] Then he makes the
cryptic statement any Calvinist would utter, "But if so, then farewell all my
comfort." Wesley responds by stating that it is the predestinarian, not the
Arminian, that is devoid of comfort:

> Then your comfort depends on a poor foundation. My comfort stands
> not on any opinion, either that a believer can or cannot fall away, not
> on the remembrance of anything wrought in me yesterday; but on what
> is today; on my present knowledge of God in Christ, reconciling me to
> himself; on my now beholding the light of the glory of God in the face
> of Jesus Christ; walking in the light as he is in the light, and having fel-
> lowship with the Father and with the Son. My comfort is, that through
> grace I now believe in the Lord Jesus Christ, and that his Spirit doth
> bear witness with my spirit that I am a child of God . . . . My rejoicing
> is this, the testimony of my conscience, that in simplicity and godly
> sincerity, not with fleshly wisdom, but by the grace of God, I have my
> conversation in the world.[114]

Here Wesley challenges the Calvinist to find "a more solid joy" than living with the daily, present reality of knowing one's sins forgiven. He is not only stressing the assurance of knowing one is saved "today," but also indicating the importance of nurturing one's relationship with Christ on a daily basis. Not that Whitefield would argue with that premise, but Wesley saw the doctrine of eternal perseverance of being a hindrance to daily holy living. If one is elected to be saved, assured of eternity in heaven, why not continue to live like "hell?" The doctrine of election, with its logical corollary, the perseverance of the saints, "wholly takes away those first motives to follow after it, so frequently proposed in Scripture, the hope of future reward and fear of punishment, the hope of heaven and fear of hell."[115] He accuses the doctrine of slamming shut the "gate" of holiness, discouraging "unholy men" from even attempting to "follow after holiness."[116]

Both Whitefield and Wesley agreed that good works should follow conversion. Yet Whitefield saw them as "privileges," things a Christian did out of obedience and love for Christ. Wesley saw them more as spiritual gauges that believers could use to check the depth of their relationship with Christ. Believers should do good works out of love and obedience, but they were also indicators of where one was in their relationship with God. "Good works," said Wesley, "are so far from being hindrances of our salvation; they are so far from being insignificant, from being of no account in Christianity; that, supposing them to spring from a right principle, they are the perfection of religion. They are the highest part of that spiritual building whereof Jesus Christ is the foundation."[117] Whitefield and Wesley agreed on the importance of good works, just not on the implications of performing them.

The Quest for Common Ground: Theological Differences?

The general consensus of interested students of the history of the eighteenth-century Evangelical Revival in England is that the two leaders came from opposite poles of the theological debate. Whitefield, the ardent Calvinist, defended the doctrines of grace while Wesley, the devoted Arminian, argued for the unlimited atonement. Perhaps this is due to the fact that "there are so many Methodists and so many Baptists" in contemporary society, and even the most casual observer, let alone a faithful member of either of these religious groups, is aware that there are basic theological differences. Many scholars agree with the conclusion that there was great disparity between Whitefield and Wesley. Historically, one's own theological predisposition determined which protagonist was supported in print.[118]

Whitefield was a Calvinist, committed to proclaiming the cherished doctrines of unconditional election, the atonement limited to the elect, and perseverance of the saints. Wesley defended his Arminian beliefs, including prevenient grace, unlimited atonement, the possibility of apostasy, and an emphasis on Christian perfection. But it is much too simplistic to boldly state that Whitefield and Wesley were worlds apart. Commitment to the authority of Scripture, the necessity of the New Birth, and justification by faith are typically viewed as points of joint agreement. These are three major points of consensus. Upon closer investigation, Whitefield and Wesley were closer than even this tri-faceted agreement suggests. Both believed that God had issued election decrees: Whitefield asserted that God had chosen who would be saved and who he would "pass by;" Wesley maintained that God had decreed, "All who believe are saved; all who do not believe are damned." Whitefield and Wesley agreed that human beings were unable to save themselves, thus the Holy Spirit had to work in the life of the person to enable the individual to respond to God. Both believed that individuals had to respond to God in faith. Each protagonist defended the importance of believers living a holy life. Whitefield and Wesley held that in one's relationship with Christ, there was firm ground for assurance that "All who believe are saved," and will be for all eternity.

Granted, this assimilation of the theological beliefs of Whitefield and Wesley overlooks certain technical issues. While both believed that individuals needed to respond to God in faith to experience regeneration, Whitefield believed that God granted faith only to the elect, while Wesley believed all humans could exercise that faith. Yet in both instances, faith was a divine gift. Whitefield and Wesley were agreed on the importance of holiness, but the former disagreed that believers could be freed from the "in-being" of sin in this life. Both believed that assurance was available for eternity, with Whitefield placing his assurance on the irrevocable decrees of God, whereas Wesley based his faith on a continual nurturing of one's relationship with God. For Wesley, as long as one "believes" and continues to "believe," that individual is assured of eternal salvation. Hence, while there were technical differences, especially differences in emphases, both men were close enough on theological grounds to cultivate evangelical ecumenicity. Concerning their evangelicalism, few would argue. As for their attempts to cultivate an evangelical consensus within the revival in general and within Methodism in particular, many would question. Overlooking differences in emphases should not have been difficult for Whitefield and Wesley in their relationship since that is exactly what they did in their relationships with believers and non-believers from many different backgrounds. To rephrase the question: How could Whitefield and Wesley cultivate "a catholic spirit" with other bodies but find it so difficult to cultivate it between themselves? Were Calvinists and Arminians from two opposite poles of the theological globe so as to be completely incompatible? What made it possible for warm relationships with some Anglicans, Congregationalists, Presbyterians, Moravians, Lutherans, Roman Catholics, and even Deists? The discussion must now address Whitefield's and Wesley's concept of theological "essentials" and "opinions;" that which was non-negotiable and that which was unimportant as a prerequisite to fellowship.

That differences existed, few would argue. That evangelical ecumenicity was unattainable, some would dispute. George Whitefield and John Wesley attained rightful positions as leaders of the Evangelical Revival in England during the eighteenth century, and as two of the most respected evangelists on two continents. Their division can be seen as a rift that has sent shockwaves through the church, the effect of which are still being felt today in the multiplication of denominations and sects. Conversely, their reunion can be viewed as a paradigm for evangelical ecumenicity beginning with eighteenth-century Methodism and continuing into the Church in the twenty-first century.

Notes

1. Stout, xiii.

2. Thomas C. Oden, *John Wesley's Scriptural Christianity* (Grand Rapids: Zondervan Publishing House, 1994), 25. Oden has highlighted Wesley's theology as systematic, in that "the gist of the whole of Wesley's theological contribution admit(s) of consistent cohesion, or general representation as a viable, organic conception and design." While admitting the "intriguing question" of how Wesley's theology developed over the years, Oden presents Wesley's "Scriptural Christianity" in the form of the standard systematic theologies.

3. George Whitefield, *Letters, 1734-1742* (Carlisle: Banner of Truth Trust, 1976), 205.

4. Ibid., 108.

5. Whitefield's journals, letters, and sermons are replete with references to these Calvinistic beliefs. They are summarized by R. Elliot, "A Summary of the Doctrine Taught by Mr. Whitefield," in George Whitefield. *Select Sermons of George Whitefield* (Carlisle, PA: The Banner of Truth Trust, 1990), 52. R. Elliot was converted under Whitefield's ministry.

6. John Wesley, *Works, Vol. VIII* (Peabody, MA: Hendrickson Publishers, Inc., 1991), 285.

7. Whitefield, *Select Sermons*, 80. The sermon "The Method of Grace" was preached from Jeremiah 6:14, "They have healed also the hurt of the daughter of my people slightly, saying, 'Peace, peace,' when there is no peace."

8. Ibid., 120. The sermon is titled, "The Lord our Righteousness," the text being Jeremiah 23:6.

9. Ibid., 120. Whitefield notes, "In this sense, and no other, are we to understand that parallel which the apostle Paul draws in the fifth of Romans, between the first and second Adam."

10. Whitefield, *Journals*, 583.

11. Whitefield, *Select Sermon*, 81.

12. Whitefield and Wesley drew different conclusions regarding the necessary effects of original sin (Wesley's argument outlined below).

13. W. Reginald Ward and Richard P. Heitzenrater, eds. *Works of John Wesley: Journals and Diaries, Vol. 21* (Nashville: Abingdon Press, 1985), 456. The letter was written on April 19, 1764. The other doctrines Wesley noted as essential to fellowship were justification by faith and holiness of heart and life.

14. Outler, ed., *Works of John Wesley: Sermons, Vol. 1*, 185.

15. Ibid., 185.

16. Ibid., 183.

17. Ibid., 183.

18. Outler, ed., *Works of John Wesley, Sermons, Vol. 2*, 423.

19. Outler, ed., *Works of John Wesley, Sermons, Vol. 4*, 302.

20. John Wesley, *Notes on the Bible* (Grand Rapids: Francis Asbury Press, 1987), 500.

21. Kenneth J. Collins, *The Scripture Way of Salvation: The Heart of John Wesley's Theology* (Nashville: Abingdon Press, 1997), 33. Collins refers to Harald Lindstrom, *Wesley and Sanctification: A Study in the Doctrine of Salvation* (Grand Rapids: Francis Asbury Press, 1980), 29. There, Lindstrom calls Adam "the representative as well as the primogenitor of mankind. When he fell, therefore, the guilt occasioned by his sin could be imputed to the whole race."

22. John Wesley, *Works, Vol. IX* (Peabody, MA: Hendrickson Publishing, 1991), 458.

23. Lindstrom, 31.

24. Collins, 34.

25. Whitefield, *Journals*, 575. This was written in the letter Whitefield wrote to Wesley after Wesley "preached and printed" his sermon on "Free Grace." Wesley's sermon and Whitefield's response give clear indication of each one's theology of election.

26. Bray, 294. The rest of the Article reads as follows: "As the godly consideration of predestination, and our election in Christ is full of sweet, pleasant and unspeakable comfort to godly persons, and such as feel in themselves the working of the Spirit of Christ, mortifying the works of the flesh and their earthly members, and drawing up their mind to high and heavenly things, as well because it doth greatly establish and confirm their faith of eternal salvation to be enjoyed through Christ, as because it doth fervently kindle their love towards God; so for curious and carnal persons, lacking the Spirit of Christ, to have continually before their eyes the sentence of God's predestination, is a most dangerous downfall, whereby the Devil doth thrust them either into desperation, or into recklessness of most unclean living, no less perilous than desperation.

"Furthermore, we must receive God's promises in such wise as they be generally set forth to us in Holy Scripture; and in our doings that will of God is to be followed which we have, expressly declared to us in the Word of God."

27. Albert C. Outler, "The Place of Wesley in the Christian Tradition," in *The Place of Wesley in the Christian Traditio: Essays delivered at Drew University in celebration of the commencement of the publication of the Oxford Edition of the Works of John Wesley*, ed. Kenneth E. Rowe (Metuchen, NJ: Scarecrow Press, 1976), 23.

28. Edward Harold Browne, *An Exposition of the Thirty-Nine Articles: Historical and Doctrinal* (London: Longmans, Green, and Co., 1865), 412.

29. Bray, 286.

30. G.F. MacLear, *An Introduction to the Articles of the Church of England* (London: Macmillan and Co., 1895), 225. Article XV affirms that the sinless Christ, by the sacrifice of himself, "should take away the sins of the world." Article XXXI asserts that "The offering of Christ once made, is the perfect redemption, propitiation, and satisfaction for the sins of the whole world, both original and actual."

31. Bray, 295.

32. E.J. Bicknell, *A Theological Introduction to the Thirty-Nine Articles of the Church of England* (London: Longmans, Green, and Co., 1961), 228. MacLear draws a similar conclusion, noting that God's "promises are to be received as they apply to all men, not to particular persons" (MacLear, 227).

33. Whitefield, *Journals*, 574.

34. John Wesley, *Works, Vol. X* (Peabody, MA: Hendrickson Publishing Co., 1991), 210.

35. Ibid, 210.

36. George Whitefield, *Letters, 1734-1742*, 89-90. The editors of this edition of Whitefield's letters suggest that the recipient of this letter was an Anglican clergyman from one of three churches of Newbury, Berkshire.

37. Oden, 243.

38. Ibid, 244. Oden quotes the Article as Wesley included it in his 1784 Articles of Religion. Wesley's Article VIII is identical to the Church of England's Article IX. Prevenient grace was not an original Methodist belief. In holding to it, Wesley continued to place himself squarely within the Anglican Church.

39. Outler, ed., *Works of John Wesley: Sermons, Vol. 3*, 203. From the sermon "On Working Out Our Own Salvation."

40. Oden, 247.

41. From letter number MCLXXXIV in George Whitefield, *Works, Vol. III.* Quoted in Stuart Clark Henry, *George Whitefield: Wayfaring Witness* (Nashville: Abingdon Press, 1957), 104.

42. Wesley, *Works, Vol. X* (Peabody, MA: Hendrickson Publishing Co., 1991), 220. Quoted in "Predestination Calmly Considered."

43. Ibid, 221.

44. Ibid., 235.

45. Ibid., 225. Wesley quotes 2 Corinthians 5:14; 1 John 2:2; and 2 Corinthians 5:15 as the scriptural backing for his belief in the unlimited atonement.

46. Randy L. Maddox, *Responsible Grace: John Wesley's Practical Theology* (Nashville: Kingswood Books, 1994).

47. Whitefield, *Select Sermons*, 100.

48. Henry, 108. Quoting Whitefield's sermon "Of Justification By Christ."

49. Gillies, 349. Whitefield's sermon on "Abraham's Offering up of His Son Isaac."

50. Ibid., 589. From his sermon "Neglect of Christ the Killing Sin."

51. Whitefield, *Select Sermons*, 100. From "Christ the Believer's Wisdom, Righteousness, Sanctification and Redemption."

52. Ibid., 100.

53. Gillies, 349. From "Abraham's Offering up His Son Isaac."

54. Whitefield, *Select Sermons*, 120. From "The Lord our Righteousness."

55. Fant, Jr., and Pinson, Jr., eds., 140. Whitefield's sermon on "Repentance and Conversion."

56. Outler, *Works of John Wesley; Sermons, Vol. 1*, 187.

57. Ibid., 189.

58. Wesley, *Works, Vol. VIII*, 361-362.

59. Collins, 79.

60. Whitefield, *Journals,* 578.

61. Wesley, *Works, Vol. X*, 313-314. From Wesley's treatise "Thoughts on Christ's Imputed Righteousness."

62. Oden, 210. Wesley feared that if individuals believed that holiness was imputed to their account, then they could be licentious, as the holiness was Christ's living in them, purifying them, thus they could live as they pleased. Wesley reviled the whole Calvinistic scheme, of which "imputed sanctification" is a part, because he believed it tended to destroy the believer's pursuit of holiness.

63. Timothy L. Smith, *Whitefield and Wesley on the New Birth* (Grand Rapids: Eerdmans, 1986), 13. Smith notes that regeneration was one of three areas in which there was almost complete agreement between Whitefield and Wesley, the other two being the authority of the Bible and the necessity of proclaiming the gospel around the world.

64. Whitefield, *Journals*, 46-47.

65. Ibid., 86. A.R. Buckland records that this was the second sermon Whitefield ever preached, and was presented for the first time at the Church of St. Mary Redcliffe, Bristol, in early 1737. A.R. Buckland, ed., *Selected Sermons of George Whitefield* (Philadelphia: The Union Press, 1904), 33.

66. Ibid., 37.

67. Ibid., 39.

68. Ibid., 43.

69. Whitefield, *Select Sermons*, 86.

70. Ibid., 103. Henry uses this quote as an illustration of Whitefield's belief in regeneration, and it does speak to being "in Christ," as Whitefield often described the New Birth. The sentence immediately preceding this quote from the sermon reads, "Thus is Christ made to believers sanctification." But for both Wesley and Whitefield, regeneration was part of the salvific process: it began with the New Birth, continued with sanctification, and culminated in ultimate salvation after death. A dramatic change indeed! See Henry, 108-110.

71. Gillies, 388. From the sermon "The Pharisee and Publican," from Luke 18:14.

72. Ibid., 579. From the sermon "Self-Inquiry Concerning the Work of God," the text being Numbers 23:23.

73. Whitefield, *Journals*, 203-204.

74. Stout, 39. Stout argues consistently that Whitefield's presentation and application to the lives of his hearers were vital ingredients in his ministry. In fact, they are two key reasons for his success.

75. Outler, ed., *Works of John Wesley; Sermons, Vol. 1*, 418-419. From the sermon "The Marks of the New Birth."

76. Ibid., 427-428.

77. Outler, ed., *Works of John Wesley; Sermons, Vol. 2*, 193-194. From the sermon "The New Birth"

78. Ibid., 193-194.

79. Outler, ed., *Works of John Wesley; Sermons, Vol. 3*, 506. From the sermon "On God's Vineyard."

80. Outler, ed., *Works of John Wesley; Sermons, Vol. 4*, 172-173. From the sermon "On Living Without God."

81. Cragg, ed., *Works of John Wesley; Vol. 11*, 107. An excerpt from "A Farther Appeal to Men of Reason and Religion."

82. Richard P. Heitzenrater and Frank Baker, eds., *Works of John Wesley: Journals, Vol. 19* (Nashville: Abingdon Press, 1990), 84. Journal entry from July 31, 1739.

83. Irwin W. Reist, "John Wesley and George Whitefield: A Study in the Integrity of Two Theologies of Grace," *Evangelical Quarterly*, 47 (1975): 34.

84. Whitefield, *Select Sermons*, 102. From "Christ, the Believer's Wisdom, Righteousness, Sanctification, and Redemption."

85. Ibid., 132.

86. Ibid., 104-105.

87. Ibid., 123. From the sermon "The Lord our Righteousness," in which Whitefield expounds his entire doctrine of the imputed righteousness of Christ.

88. Fant, Jr., and Pinson, Jr., 140.

89. John Wesley, *Works, Vol. XI* (Peabody, MA: Hendrickson Publishing Co., 1991), 387. From Wesley's *Plain Account of Christian Perfection*.

90. Ibid., 387.

91. Ibid., 394.

92. Ibid., 417.

93. Ibid., 441-442.

94. Ibid., 442.

95. Ibid., 446. This earlier writing is an abridgment of his interpretation of the doctrine, *Brief Thoughts on Christian Perfection*, from January 27, 1767.

96. Oden, 199.

97. Outler, ed., *Works of John Wesley: Sermons, Vol. 1*, 187. Wesley's sermon "Justification By Faith."

98. Richard P. Heitzenrater, *Wesley and the People Called Methodists* (Nashville: Abingdon Press, 1995), 107.

99. Oden, 313.

100. Smith, 24.

101. Ibid., 24.

102. Obviously, it is impossible to know whether Whitefield was consciously quoting Wesley's sermons, or his New Testament notes on Acts 1:5, where the language is also employed. Yet the circumstantial evidence is intriguing.

103. Leon O. Hynson, "George Whitefield and Wesleyan Perfectionism: A Response," *The Wesleyan Theological Journal*, 19 (Spring 1984): 87.

104. Ibid., 88-89.

105. Whitefield, *Select Sermons*, 106.

106. Whitefield, *Letters*, 209.

107. Ibid., 209.

108. Ibid., 214. Smith notes these two letters as important pieces of the sanctification dispute between Wesley and Whitefield. See Smith, 20-21.

109. Whitefield, *Journals*, 578.

110. Ibid., 580.

111. Ibid., 581.

112. Wesley, *Works, Vol. VIII*, 277.

113. Wesley, *Works, Vol. X*, 285. Wesley cites Psalm 89:30-35; 1 Timothy 1:18-19; Romans 11:17, 20-22; and John 15:1-6, among others that appear to indicate the necessity of the believer "remaining" or "abiding" in Christ.

114. Ibid., 295.

115. Outler, ed. *Works of John Wesley: Sermons, Vol. 3*, 548. From the sermon "Free Grace."

116. Ibid., 548.

117. Ibid., 405. From the sermon "The Reward of Righteousness."

118. This was occurring during the days of Whitefield and Wesley and continues to the present day. Early on, Wesley was backed by his brother and John Fletcher, Whitefield supported by Howell Harris, Augustus Toplady, and numerous American allies. Later, Wesley was defended by Luke Tyerman; Whitefield by Arnold Dallimore. Recent scholarship has been more effective at treating each man more fairly.

Chapter 3

The Quest for Common Ground
Outside Methodism

It is insufficient to state that Whitefield, Wesley, and those with whom they differed simply "agreed to disagree." Even if this was the final outcome of the matter, there had to be contributing causes to the initial debate. Wesley and Whitefield clearly indicated that there were certain theological basics, "essentials," upon which there was no room for debate. Throughout his *Journals*, Whitefield reinforced the "necessity of the new birth," often coupled with "justification by faith alone." Wesley affirmed the vital nature of these two doctrines. This also raises the question concerning the basis upon which the agreement could be founded. Coppedge has suggested that "the line of demarcation was the Scripture."[1] Even if this was the case for Wesley, was it true for Whitefield? Were those with whom both men sought fellowship acceptable under this proposed framework? Were there other issues at work? An examination of both men's relationships with other believers is vital to this understanding. Both had vast networks of friendships, some of which spanned two continents. Each one claimed to possess a "catholic spirit" that was essential to the building of an evangelical consensus to extend the work of the Evangelical Revival.

The concept of a "catholic spirit" lies at the heart of understanding the relationship between Wesley and Whitefield and their relationships with other Christians. Far from advocating narrow sectarianism, both leaders of early Methodism endeavored to cultivate connections with other "warm hearted" believers of varying denominations. Both also guarded against the other extreme — unquestioning acceptance of any and all theological innovation. "Evangelical ecumenicity" best captures the essence of the "catholic spirit" each was attempting to foster. The challenges lay in promoting evangelical ecumenicity, retaining their theological integrity, and doing so to continue the successes of the Evangelical Revival.

Relations with the Church of England

Justifying grace had made John Wesley and George Whitefield children of God. Ordination had made them priests of the Church of England. Neither ever renounced, nor were stripped of, their holy orders. In the spirit of the Reformers, both believed that the Church of England could be reformed from within, and could be the means whereby God would begin another general reforming of the Church. Yet these two sons of Canterbury had, at one time or another, cordial, neutral, and strained relations with their ecclesiastical family.

Ordained into the Anglican priesthood in 1736 at age twenty-one, Whitefield did not enter orders "unadvisedly or lightly." He spent the days prior to his ordination in serious preparation for his final examination. "I strictly examined myself by the qualifications required for a minister in St. Paul's Epistle to Timothy, and also by every question that I knew was to be publicly put to me at the time of my ordination." Subsequent days were spent in study, fasting, and prayer. On Trinity Sunday, Whitefield wrote of his ordination: "When the bishop laid his hands upon my head, my heart was melted down, and I offered up my whole spirit, soul and body to the service of God's sanctuary. I read the Gospel, at the bishop's command, with power, and afterwards sealed the good confession I had made before many witnesses, by partaking of the Holy Sacrament."[2] The high esteem in which he held his calling was evident, not simply by his affirmation of it, but by the fervor with which he attacked his clerical responsibilities. Within weeks he accepted invitations to officiate in the absence of curates in London and Dummer.

From the start, Whitefield made full use of his orders. He continued to use his Anglican ordination to defend his itinerant ministry. As early as 1737, he asked the Bishop of London if his ministry necessitated a special license. The Bishop replied in the negative.[3] Two years later, during a preaching tour in Gloucester, Whitefield bemoaned the fact that some "forbid" him to "speak to these poor baptized heathens that they may be saved." He challenged his accusers to defend their case with arguments that will not merely satisfy clerical reasoning, but would stand up under divine scrutiny:

> I am, and profess myself, a member of the Church of England. I have received no prohibition from any of the Bishops; and having had no fault found by them with my life or doctrine, have the same general license to preach which the rectors are willing to think sufficient for their curates; nor can any of them produce one instance of their having refused the assistance of a stranger clergyman, because he had not a written license. And have their lordships, the Bishops, insisted that no person shall ever preach occasionally without such special license? Is not our producing our letters or Orders always judged sufficient? Have not some of us been allowed to preach in Georgia, and other places, by no other than our general commission? . . . His lordship of London allowed of my preaching there, even when I had only received Deacon's Orders; and I have never been charged by his lordship with teaching or living otherwise than as a true minister of the Church of England.[4]

Within two weeks, he was denied a pulpit in Islington, as he had no license from the bishop. He mused that as possessor of the living at Savannah, within the bishopric of London, he had "a stronger license than that implicit one by which hundreds of the inferior clergy are by his lordship permitted to preach."[5] He did not press the issue, but later preached in the churchyard. In a letter penned that day he tersely noted, "I always hope well of opposers. Today, my master by his providence and spirit compelled me to preach in the church-yard at Islington."[6] He employed the same defense in New York in November 1739 when denied the pulpit of Commissary Vessey. Whitefield argued:

> . . . I never heard that the Bishop of London gave any license to any one who went to preach the Gospel in Georgia; but that I was presented to the living of Savannah by the trustees, and upon that presentation had letters Dismissory from my lord of London, which I thought was sufficient authority.[7]

In characteristic fashion, Whitefield attempted to deflect the attack on the propriety of his preaching in parishes not his own by charging his accuser with behavior unbecoming a clergyman, namely, frequenting public houses. For Whitefield, it did not make sense for a clergyman to prevent him from preaching the gospel while the same clergyman's lifestyle was inconsistent with ministerial deportment. Elsewhere he lamented, "I have no objection against, but highly approve of the excellent Liturgy of our Church, would ministers lend me their churches to use it in."[8]

Whitefield did not consider leaving the Church of England nor would he counsel those affected by his ministry to separate. In April 1739, it came to Whitefield's attention that several of his followers in Oxford were in various stages of separating from the Church. Charles Kinchin, one of the priests for whom Whitefield had briefly substituted following his ordination, was considering the resignation of his living. Whitefield confessed that this news gave him a "great shock:"

> For I knew what dreadful consequences would attend a needless separation from the Established Church. For my own part, I can see no reason for my leaving the Church, however I am treated by the corrupt members and ministers of it. I judge of the state of a Church, not from the practice of its members, but its primitive and public constitutions; and so long as I think the Articles of the Church of England are agreeable to Scripture, I am resolved to preach them up without either bigotry or party zeal. For I love all who love the Lord Jesus.[9]

On April 22, Whitefield wrote to Kinchin, imploring him to reconsider his decision to separate. It was an idea that Whitefield was convinced was of diabolical origin. He warned Kinchin of the "confusion" his separation from the Church would propagate, reminding him that "most are afraid almost to converse with us." It was Whitefield's contention that his "being a minister of the Church of England, and preaching its Articles, is a means, under God, of drawing so many after me."[10] Whitefield's letter to Kinchin reveals several characteristics of his relationship with the Church of England. First, he fully believed himself to be a faithful son of the Church. His preaching of the doctrines he believed evident in the Articles of Faith was the means of bringing many to faith. He also had no problem accepting even the vestments and rubrics of the Church. Writing to Kinchin he exclaimed, "As for objecting about the habits, robes, &c., good God! I thought we long since knew that the Kingdom of God did not consist in any externals, but in righteousness, and peace, and joy in the Holy Ghost." Finally, Whitefield affirmed that separation from the Church was not an option. In fact, toward the end of this stay at Oxford, in the wake of the Kinchin incident, Whitefield exhorted "all the brethren not to forsake the assembling themselves together . . . for so long as they continued steadfast in the communion of the Established Church, I told them no power on earth could justify hindering them from continuing in fellowship . . . "[11]

On another occasion, Whitefield endeavored to persuade an Anglican clergyman to remain within the Church and to recapture the spirit of the Thirty-Nine Articles in his preaching. "O pity, pity the church of England," cries Whitefield. "See how too, too many of her sons are fallen from her articles, and preach themselves, not Christ Jesus the Lord." He encourages his correspondent to pray for more faithful witnesses to arise from within the Church, and prays, "Oh that dear Mr. T. may be one of them! . . . Arise, arise, and be not of the number of those who only fleece their flocks . . . . I long to have the pure scripture truths, as delivered in our homilies and our articles, preached up universally."[12]

It is evident that Whitefield was committed to fulfilling his ordination vows to the Church of England as he understood them. He was also not above emphasizing his relationship to the Church when it would benefit his ministry, though his general attitude toward the Church was to minimize his connectedness. He could downplay his relationship to the Church to such an extent as to have fraternal relationships with those who had limited or even no relationship with the Church of England.

John Wesley wrote truthfully in 1790, "I live and die a member of the Church of England." This was a statement that Whitefield could just as well have written.[13] While an unsympathetic Knox suggests that Wesley was the one responsible for strained relations with the Church of England, Wesley counted himself a faithful son of the Church until his death.[14] Evidence for Wesley's contention is abundant. Only months after his Aldersgate experience, Wesley edited an abridgment of the first five of the *Edwardian Homilies*, the standard sermons of the Church of England. The resulting work, *The Doctrine of*

Salvation, Faith and Good Works, Extracted from the Homilies of the Church of England, indicates that Wesley, at an early point in his "evangelical" career, fully supported the teachings of the *Homilies*. His numerous abridgments did little to mar the theological beliefs intended by the original author(s), but as Outler suggests, were simply meant "to excise every passage in Cranmer that could be eliminated without mangling the nerve of the argument."[15] Thus Wesley agreed with Cranmer:

> In these places the apostle toucheth especially on three things which must go together in our justification: upon God's part, his great mercy and grace; upon Christ's part, the satisfaction of God's justice by the offering his body and shedding his blood, with the fulfilling of the law perfectly and thoroughly; and upon our part, true and lively faith in the merits of Jesus Christ[16]

> And (that we are) justified only by this true and lively faith in Christ speak all the ancient authors, especially Origen, St. Cyprian, St. Chrysostom, Hilary, Basil, St. Ambrose and St. Augustine, by which they take away clearly all merit of our works and wholly ascribe our justification unto Christ only. This faith, the Holy Scripture teacheth us, is the strong rock and foundation of the Christian religion. This doctrine all ancient authors of Christ's church do approve. This doctrine setteth forth the true glory of Christ and beateth down the vainglory of man.[17]

Did Wesley have ulterior motives for encouraging Methodists to remain in the Church of England? Rack suggests:

> Ties with the church were valued not for theoretical but practical reasons: to avoid divisions within Methodism and to avoid creating a localizing sect. It was not so much an obsession with "order" that kept him in the church as the failure of the church to thrust him out that preserved Methodism from separation. Despite his ingenious distinctions, Wesley opposed separation as inexpedient rather than unlawful, and clearly allowed that he would separate rather than give up his system. One may well conclude that for all his skilful manoeuvering it was the failure of the authorities to expel him that enable him proudly to "live and die in the Church of England." To do so at all costs was certainly not his aim.[18]

Wesley's outlook could be interpreted in this light. In his *Reasons Against a Separation from the Church of England*, he declared, "Whether it be lawful or no . . . it is by no means expedient, for us to separated from the established

Church."[19] And yet, upon closer examination of Wesley's reasoning defending this statement, it becomes clear that Rack's and Wesley's interpretations of "expediency" are two different things. Wesley's defense of the "inexpediency" of separation was based on his conviction that the integrity of the Methodist movement must be preserved. He argued that separation would contradict the Methodist's "repeated declarations" that they would remain within the Church. Further, it would give ammunition to the "enemies of God" to rightfully accuse the Methodists of being less than honest. Separation would prevent many who love God from listening further to their message and would hinder the uncommitted from giving ear as well. Additionally, separatist Methodists would be alienated from non-separatist Methodists, and strife would arise between non-Methodist Anglicans and Methodists. Wesley's time would be occupied with the ensuing controversy rather than with preaching, and establishing a new Church would require more time, care, and expertise than any of the current Methodist leaders possessed. Besides, other attempts at establishing new Churches had failed, after all, and the Dissenters had been largely unsuccessful. But Wesley firmly believed that God had called the Methodists to reform the Church of England, not to leave it![20] Hence, while Wesley would not comment on the legality of separation, he believed it was not "expedient," as he had a divine mandate to remain part of the Church of England. It may not have been against the laws of man, but it certainly was against the will of God. Until God redirected, the Methodists would remain the most faithful members of the established Church.

Wesley's series of *Appeals to Men of Reason and Religion* was written to respond to many of the indictments lodged against the Methodists, including those that marked them as "enthusiasts," "Papists," and "schismatics." Charging Wesley with advocating separation from the Church, what one accuser termed "schism," was sure to bring a calculated response. In *A Farther Appeal, Part III*, Wesley argued that those who responded to the Methodist message in no wise separated from the Church. He contended that those who never attended the services of the Church were now regular attenders. Those who rarely went to worship "are united to it more closely than before." But for Wesley, the ultimate defense was:

> . . . are they turned from doing the works of the devil to do the works of God? Do they now live soberly, righteously, and godly in the present world? If they do, if they live according to the directions of the Church, believe her doctrines, and join in her ordinances — with what face can you say that these men separate from the Church of England?[21]

Previously, in *An Earnest Appeal to Men of Reason and Religion*, Wesley replied to accusations of leaving the Church. He questioned how anyone could suggest such a ludicrous incrimination. How had the Methodists left the Church? By going outside of the walls of church buildings? In departing from the fundamental doctrines of the Church? Were their practices contrary to those of the established Church? The questions were rhetorical but the answers were plain. The accusation of divisiveness was countered with Wesley's typical flair:

> We "divide them," you say, "by uniting them together." Truly a very uncommon way of dividing! O, but we divide those who are thus united with each other from the rest of the Church. By no means. Many of them were before "joined to all their brethren" of the Church of England (and many were not until they knew us) by "assembling themselves together" to hear the Word of God, and to eat of one bread and drink of one cup. And do they now "forsake that assembling themselves together?" You cannot, you dare not, say it. You know they are more diligent therein than ever, it being one of the fixed rules of our societies, that every member attend the ordinances of God, i.e. that he do not divide from the Church. And if any member of the Church does divide from or leave it he hath no more place among us.[22]

Far from being schismatic, the Methodists were the "glue" holding the Church together, in spite of other influences that were attempting to tear her apart. "We are now defending the Church, even the Church of England, in opposition to all those who either secretly undermine or openly attempt to destroy it."[23] Some of Wesley's sharpest attacks were leveled against those clergy within the Church of England that he viewed as the true schismatics. These were those clerics who, while ordained by the Church, were not being true to the cherished doctrines of the Church, especially that of justification by faith. Such members of the clergy were "practically separating" from the Church, while the Methodists were not.[24] Wesley had concluded that "the whole tenor" of the Church's "Liturgy, Articles and Homilies" affirmed that "no good work, properly so called, can go before justification," and that the "meritorious cause of justification is the life and death of Christ," while the "condition of it is faith, faith alone."[25]

The Methodists were preaching what the Church historically believed, while much of the clergy had abandoned sound doctrine. Referencing Article XIX, Wesley notes "three things essential to a visible church:" living faith, preaching of the pure Word of God, and due administration of the sacraments.[26] The Methodists were not the ones diminishing these in any way; in fact, deference to them among the Methodists was on the increase. Wesley was amazed at the irony surrounding the Anglican clergy, whose ranks were dotted with "drunkards, gluttons, returners of evil for evil, liars, swearers, and profaners of the day of the Lord," yet who criticized the Methodists for "irregularities" such as field preaching. He highlights the case of Rev. John Romley, who accused him of not being fit to receive communion, assumedly for having preached from his father's tombstone in the churchyard. Yet the verbally abusive Romley was "seen fit" to administer the sacrament.[27]

Wesley viewed himself as a faithful son of the Church of England who would honestly assess her spirituality and recommend changes that needed to be made. In doing so, Wesley always reaffirmed his connectedness to the Church. The motives of the Church of England and the Methodists were, in Wesley's view, identical:

> Now cannot you join in all this? . . . O when will you take knowledge that our whole concern, our constant labour, is to bring all the world to the religion which you feel, to solid, inward, vital religion. What power is it then that keeps us asunder? . . . No differences between us (if thou art a child of God) can be so considerable as our agreement is. If we differ in smaller things, we agree in that which is greatest of all.[28]

And further:

> We do not dispute concerning any of the externals or circumstantials of religion. There is no room; for we agree with you therein . . . . (Dissenters, including Quakers, Presbyterians, and Baptists) spend a great part of their time and strength in contending about externals and circumstantials: we agree with you in both; so that having no room to spend any time in such vain contention, we have our desire of spending and being spent in promoting plain, practical religion.[29]

According to Wesley, to link the Methodists to the Dissenters was inappropriate. While most Dissenting bodies claimed that "at the Church we are fed with chaff," Wesley argued that the prayers, the Eucharist, the doctrine, and even many of the sermons heard in the Church of England were not "chaff." Those who are "alive to God" will find more than adequate nourishment from the feeding received in the established Church.[30] Even late in his life, Wesley still held the liturgy of his Church in high regard. He wrote to Miss Bishop, ". . . I myself find more life in the Church Prayers than in any formal extemporary prayers of Dissenters. Nay, I find more profit in sermons on either good tempers, or good works, than in what are vulgarly called Gospel sermons."[31] Later still, he noted in his *Preface to the Sunday Service of the Methodists in the United States of America*:

> I believe there is no Liturgy in the world, either in ancient or modern language, which breathes more of a solid, scriptural, rational piety, than

the Common Prayer of the Church of England: And though the main of
it was compiled considerably more than two hundred years ago, yet is
the language of it not only pure, but strong and elegant in the highest
degree.[32]

Wesley never left the Church of England because he believed it to be the
soundest, most biblically based Church on earth. While quick to shine the light
into its dark corners, he understood that the "darkness could not overcome the
light." So adamant was Wesley that he and the Methodists were the most faithful
of Anglicans, that when Bishop Gibson advised them to "have a greater regard
to the rules and order of the Church," Wesley responded, "I cannot; for I now
regard them next to the Word of God. And as to your last: 'to renounce
communion with the Church,' I dare not. Nay, but let them thrust us out. We
will not leave the ship: if you cast us out of it, then our Lord will take us up."[33]

Both Wesley and Whitefield died as members of the clergy of the Church of
England. Both had their opportunities to discontinue fellowship, but both held
onto the hope that the Church could be reformed from within. Each one suffered
attacks from the establishment, and used the press and the pulpit to counter each
offensive. They believed that they could remain members of the Church of
England and still preach experiential religion. Their relationships with individual
members of the Church of England were strained, but they never crossed into
heterodoxy as to be "cast out" by the Church hierarchy. They found in the
Church of England enough room to maintain their individual theological
integrity and to continue the work of the revival. Accordingly, it is not
surprising that, as members of the same denomination, Whitefield and Wesley
would be largely in agreement on basic issues. The groundwork for an
evangelical consensus was laid, which makes their disagreement all that more
difficult to comprehend. What is even more puzzling is how both could carry on
cordial relationships with those of differing theological viewpoints, yet have
such a wrenching separation between themselves.

Relations with Quakers

Whitefield's catholic spirit extended to members of the Society of Friends.
He had occasion to dialogue with them in both England and North America, and
those meetings were marked by cordial discourse. This is not to suggest that
Whitefield was in complete agreement with his Quaker acquaintances.[34] He
appreciated much that he saw in the demeanor and beliefs of the Friends. On
March 23, 1739, he wrote, "Dined with many Quakers at Frenchay, who
entertained me and my friends with much Christian love."[35] He frequently
commended them for their hospitality during his travels. Whitefield fondly
remembered courteous Quakers of Clapham, "where he dined;"[36] an "eminent

Quaker in Bath, who entertained me and my friends in a most Christian manner;"[37] a "Friend's house" in Bristol, "where we ate our bread with gladness and singleness of heart;"[38] at Thornbury, where he "breakfasted;"[39] and at Basingstoke, "At whose house I lodged."[40] He spoke of "two loving Quakers" who provided lodging for him on a trip from Chester, Pennsylvania, to Wilmington, Delaware.[41] Months later he noted, "After sermon, I and my friends dined at a Quakers, who seemed to have a right spirit within him, and could speak as one experienced in the things of God."[42] On another trip through Pennsylvania, Whitefield wrote of his stay in St. George's, "where a kind and courteous Quaker received us into his house."[43] In at least two letters, Whitefield commended the Quakers as examples of how Christians should endure suffering. Writing from a staunchly Quaker Philadelphia, Whitefield noted, "The Quakers . . . have left us an example of patient suffering, and did more by their bold, unanimous and persevering testimonies, than if they had taken up all the arms in the kingdom."[44] He wrote to Charles Wesley only weeks prior, "The Quakers have set us an example of patient, resolute suffering, as the best means to weary our enemies."[45]

Yet while Whitefield appreciated the hospitality of numerous Quakers in an age when itinerants had to depend on the courtesy of strangers, and could find enough to commend in the Society of Friends, he could not endorse many of their theological beliefs. To "a friend in London" he wrote from New Brunswick, New Jersey, on April 27, 1740, "The bigoted, self-righteous Quakers now also begin to spit out a little of the venom of the serpent. They cannot bear the doctrine of original sin, and of an imputed righteousness as the cause of our acceptance with God. One of their head teachers called original sin original nonsense."[46] He affirmed that Quaker "notions about walking and being led by the Spirit are right and good," but could not agree with them on discarding the use of the sacraments nor on their refusal of paying the tithe.[47] While extolling them for the catholic spirit they exhibited, he found that Quaker arguments against the outward call to the ministry were not "at all convincing."[48] Whitefield was accompanied by a "Quaker preacher" on his voyage from England to North America in the fall of 1739. After lending his cabin to his Quaker colleague one Sunday in September, Whitefield recorded:

> He spoke with much earnestness, but in my opinion his foundation was wrong. He seemed to make the light of conscience, and the Holy Spirit, one and the same thing, and represented Christ within, and not Christ without, as the foundation of our faith; whereas, the outward righteousness of Jesus Christ, imputed to us, I believe, is the sole fountain and cause of all the inward communications which we receive from the Spirit of God. Oh, that all of that persuasion were convinced of this; till they are, they cannot preach the truth as it is in Jesus.[49]

During his subsequent stay in Philadelphia, Whitefield attended a Quaker meeting, commenting that he "felt somewhat in sympathy" with the speaker. "But I heartily wish that they would talk of an outward as well as an inward Christ; for otherwise, we make our own holiness, and not the righteousness of Jesus Christ the cause of our being accepted by God. From such doctrine may I always turn away."[50] Reflecting on his stay in Philadelphia, Whitefield expounds on the Quaker majority:

> I fear numbers amongst them, as amongst us, can give no other reason why they are Quakers, than that their fathers were so before them. I say this, because I find little of Divine Power stirring amongst them; and most of them are too stiff and rigid about external things, I was credibly informed. One of their own preachers warned them lately of their backsliding, and told them, that without a reformation, God would remove the candlestick from them, and work no more by their hands. In the city of Philadelphia they have two large meeting-houses, where they assemble frequently together; and, all things considered, are the most regular society of men I have seen or heard of.[51]

Whitefield could not abide by spiritual lukewarmness, whether he found it in his own Church or another. But for those who were spiritually enlightened, Whitefield had a place in his ministry. He included in his *Journals* a letter from a Quaker at Basingstoke with whom he had boarded. The rather uncharacteristic evangelical testimony of the Quaker was reproduced by Whitefield in its entirety. It read, in part:

> O thy noble testimony against the profaneness and vanity of the age! It rejoiced me not a little. But when thou camest to the necessity, the nature, and the rewards of the new birth, thou wert carried beyond thyself. I, for one, am a monument of free grace and mercy . . . . I have often drunk of the spiritual Rock, and been a witness of the joys of God's salvation; of that sweet presence of Christ, which carries men above the fear of the world, and enables them to overcome the world; that baptiseth into the spirit and nature of the Son of God, and maketh disciples indeed. It is a sense of God ever near, the influences of His quickening Spirit, that is only able to deter from evil, crucify the old nature, create again to God, and perform His good and acceptable will. This will make a thorough reformation, beginning at the heart, sanctifying it, guarding it, and making it a holy temple for the Holy Spirit to dwell in; then producing holy thoughts, longings after Divine enjoyments, love, joy, solidity, watchfulness, &c.[52]

Whitefield could also praise warmhearted religion wherever he found it. And he was more than willing to introduce awakened Quakers to the sacraments of the Church of England. At the Church of St. Mary de Crypt, Gloucester, on April 17, 1739, Whitefield baptized "a professed Quaker, about sixty years of age, who was convinced of the necessity of being born of water, as well as the Spirit."[53] Later that spring, Whitefield sent two "convinced" Quakers to be baptized by Mr. Stonehouse.[54] In a fascinating series of instances, Whitefield, a member of the Anglican clergy "born of the Spirit," sent several converted Quakers to another Anglican vicar who had experienced the New Birth. This illustrated not only Whitefield's willingness to work with like-minded colleagues within the Church of England, but also revealed his openness to those outside of Anglican circles who witnessed to experiential faith.

In a letter dated February 10, 1747, John Wesley answered correspondence from a Quaker who asked, "Is there any difference between Quakerism and Christianity?" Wesley believed that there was. He proceeds to outline the differences as "plainly as he can."[55] The basic premises of the Society of Friends and the Christianity of the Church of England contained no differences. Both hold that the true knowledge of God is the key to human happiness, and that this true knowledge of God has been revealed to humanity through the Holy Spirit. But Wesley quoted Robert Barclay, Quaker divine, as saying that "these revelations are not to be subjected to the examination of the Scriptures as to a touchstone."[56] Wesley could not agree. He argued, "Here there is a difference. The Scriptures are the touchstone whereby Christians examine all, real or supposed revelations. In all cases they appeal 'to the law and to the testimony,' and try every spirit thereby."[57] The self-proclaimed *homo unius libri* based his theology squarely in the pages of the Christian Scriptures.

Quakers further argued that the Scriptures were not "the principal ground of all truth and knowledge, nor the adequate, primary rule of faith and manners . . . they are a secondary rule, subordinate to the Spirit."[58] Wesley agreed that the Spirit was the principal leader, but that the Scriptures could still be referred to as the rule that led to truth. "Call the Spirit our guide," Wesley suggests, "which signifies an intelligent being, and the Scriptures our rule, which signifies something used by an intelligent being, and all is plain and clear."[59]

Wesley not only rejected the Quaker diminution of the importance of Scripture. He also rebuffed many of their liturgical beliefs and practices. He characterized Quakers as believing that since only the Holy Spirit can "incline one to worship," all true worship must be precipitated by the "inward and immediate moving" of the Holy Spirit. Thus carefully prepared sermons and scripted prayers were considered "superstitious, will-worship, and abominable idolatry in the sight of God," hence not true worship. Such arguments put the churchman Wesley on the defensive. He argued that God wills for humanity to worship, and while one may not always "feel led" to do so, obedience demands it.

God moves man, whom he has made a reasonable creature, according to the reason which he has given him. He moves him by his understanding, as well as his affections; by light, as well as by heat . . . Prove me that proposition, if you can: "Every man who preaches or prays at an appointed time, preaches or prays in his own will, and not by the Spirit" . . . . In truth, from the beginning to the end, you set this matter upon a wrong foundation. It is not on this circumstance, — the being at set times or not, that the acceptableness of our prayers depends; but on the intention and tempers with which we pray. He that prays in faith, at whatsoever time, is heard.[60]

Wesley deepened his liturgical debate with the Quakers by calling into question their dependence on "silence" during worship. The Anglican faithful, whose senses were fully involved in the various aspects of the liturgy, could not defend the Quaker insistence on refraining from all outward expressions of faith, until compelled by the Spirit. Wesley dismissed it bluntly by calling it "will-worship, if there be any such thing under heaven."[61] "Waiting" and "stillness" for Wesley included "waiting" by employing the means of grace made available to the Church. When Quakers argued against outward baptism, stating that the "one baptism" referred to in Scripture was an inward baptism, Wesley stood by the Anglican practice of one outward baptism. Quakers who argued that the Lord's Supper was merely a figure that "ceases in such as have obtained the substance," Wesley argued for the plain meaning of the Scriptures, "Do this in remembrance of me," and "As often as ye eat and drink . . ."[62] In fact, it was at this point that Wesley found the greatest disagreement between the Quakers and himself. He wrote to his regular correspondent, John Smith, on June 25, 1746, "between me and them (Quakers) there is a great gulf fixed. The sacraments of baptism and the Lord's Supper keep us at a wide distance from each other; insomuch that, according to the view of things I have now, I should as soon commence Deist as Quaker."[63]

Yet, while acknowledging a "great gulf" that existed separating Anglican sensibilities from Quaker stillness, Wesley spoke fondly of numerous Quakers he encountered. During a particularly emotional period of revival in Bristol, Wesley wrote that one Quaker "was not a little displeased" at the emotionalism. Eventually, however, even he was affected and declared of Wesley, "Now I know thou art a prophet of the Lord."[64] Later that same year, Wesley recorded the account of a conversation held with a Quaker and an Anabaptist, both of whom he described as having "a large measure of the love of God shed abroad in their hearts." He concluded with a hopeful prayer, "O may those, in every persuasion, who are of this spirit, increase a thousand-fold, how many soever they be!"[65] Early in 1740, it was rumored that Wesley had invited Quaker Joseph Chandler to a public debate. It was also said that Chandler promised to attend, but never made an appearance. Instead of believing the rumor being circulated, Chandler sent a messenger to Wesley to determine the truth. Of Chandler's integrity, Wesley noted, "If those who probably count themselves better Christians had but done like this honest Quaker, how many idle tales, which they now potently believe, would, like this, have vanished into air!"[66]

Wesley, like Whitefield, was alert to the Spirit of God dwelling in believers of other denominations, as witnessed on a September 1743 trip through Sticklepath. Wesley was stopped and asked if he was John Wesley. Upon confirmation, others arrived, encouraging him to stay. Wesley continued, ". . . before we had spoke many words, our souls took acquaintance with each other. I found they were called Quakers; but that hurt not me; seeing the love of God was in their hearts."[67] The awareness of the Spirit dwelling in Wesley was also witnessed by Quakers. After Wesley preached in the churchyard at Leominster, a Quaker followed him to his lodgings. He was "much displeased" with Wesley over his last *Appeal*, but he continued, "my displeasure is gone: I heard thee speak, and my heart clave to thee."[68] Wesley also spoke fondly of John Garret, "one of the most lovely old men I ever saw . . . a Dutchman by birth, and a Speaker among the Quakers,"[69] and another Quaker whom he referred to as one who "spoke in the very spirit and language wherein poor Mr. Hall used to speak, before he made shipwreck of the grace of God. I found it good to be with him: It enlivened and strengthened my soul."[70] Undoubtedly, Wesley found rewarding the numerous Quaker "converts" that he baptized.[71]

However, for the vast literary output of John Wesley, the limited amount of praise for members of the Society of Friends suggests that Wesley had more difficulty overlooking the theological differences he had with the Quakers than did Whitefield. As we have discovered, Whitefield differed with the Quakers on original sin, hypocrisy, and stillness. Interestingly, Whitefield offered high praise for Pennsylvania, North America's Quaker stronghold. Of Pennsylvania, Whitefield wrote, "To me it seems to be the garden of America . . . all are permitted to worship God their own way, without being branded as schismatics, dissenters, or disturbers of the established constitution."[72] Whitefield found in Pennsylvania, not only a colony where his message was welcomed, but also one of his most successful mission fields and publishing headquarters. The pragmatic results that accompanied life in Quaker Pennsylvania were of greater importance to Whitefield than the theological differences he had with the Quakers. For Wesley, results were important indeed, but not at the expense of theological integrity.

The key point of agreement between Wesley and the Quakers was the issue of slavery. While Whitefield could own slaves and support the institution with a clear conscience, Wesley was strongly opposed. Following his typical pattern of "reading, borrowing, editing, supplementing, and expanding," Wesley wrote his *Thoughts upon Slavery* depending heavily on Judge William Blackstone and Quaker Anthony Benezet.[73] A devoted Quaker abolitionist, Benezet had published several tracts and a more extensive book on slavery by the time

Wesley was introduced to him.[74] Having found a kindred spirit, Wesley "borrowed, edited, supplemented, and expanded" Benezet's contribution to the argument against slavery. Up to 75% of Wesley's *Thoughts upon Slavery* was directly borrowed from Benezet.[75] Wesley was always willing to employ the truth, no matter what the source.

For Wesley as for Whitefield, simply being a Quaker did not mean an automatic cessation of spiritual fellowship. Once again, the key factor was one's "heart relationship" with God. If the Quaker had experienced saving faith, Whitefield and Wesley were more than cordial in their relationships with them. If, however, the Quaker held beliefs that were accounted unscriptural, the rhetoric employed, especially by Wesley, became more pointed. Evangelical ecumenicity could be achieved even with Quakers, but only with Quakers who had a right understanding of the "inward principle" as interpreted by the Methodists. Wesley summarizes it this way:

> Friend, you have an honest heart, but a weak head . . . . Once your zeal was against ungodliness and unrighteousness, against evil tempers and evil works. Now it is against forms of prayer, against singing psalms or hymns, against appointing times of praying or preaching; against saying "you" to a single person, uncovering your head, or having too many buttons upon your coat. O what a fall is here! What poor trifles are these, that now well-nigh engross your thoughts! Come back, come back, to the weightier matters of the law, to spiritual, rational, scriptural religion.[76]

Had all Dissenters and loyal churchmen heeded this cry, the evangelical ecumenicity Whitefield and Wesley sought would have become a reality.

Relations with Moravians

Of all the relationships that George Whitefield and John Wesley nurtured, those with followers of the Moravians should have been the easiest to cultivate. The Moravians and both Whitefield and Wesley were firmly rooted in the Pietist heritage, a warm-hearted, experiential spiritual heritage. Given the important influence that the Moravians had on Wesley's early spiritual development, one would assume that evangelical ecumenicity with them would be a foregone conclusion.[77] Yet the controversy that arose with Zinzendorf and the Moravians was nearly as heated as that which developed between Calvinistic evangelicals and Wesleyan Methodists.

Whitefield's dealings with Moravians were highlighted by a few references among his letters and journal entries and one major business dealing. As illustrated in his relationships with individuals from other denominations,

Whitefield allowed for some difference of opinion while focusing on fundamental similarities, especially those relating to justification by faith. In a letter to James Habersham, Whitefield indicated that some from Philadelphia had suspicions that Whitefield had affiliated with the Moravians. He assured Habersham that this is not the case, and noted, "My principles are still the same; only as I believe many of (the Moravians) love the Lord Jesus, I would love and be friendly to them, as I would be to all others, who I think bear the image of our common Master, notwithstanding some of my principles differ from theirs, and are as far distant as the East is from the West."[78]

Elsewhere Whitefield shed light on which principles he and the Moravians differed. Already in 1740, he was concerned to have discovered that "some English friends had thrown aside the use of means," apparently a reference to the Moravian controversy in which the Fetter Lane Society was embroiled.[79] Within months, Whitefield wrote to Mr. C.G., accusing him of perverting the Scripture, "Be still, and know that I am the Lord." Whitefield feared his correspondent had fallen into "false stillness," much like Whitefield himself had practiced during his Oxford days, abstaining from "writing, reading, and such like exercises." He admonished, "You say, 'Be still' (Our Savior) says, 'Strive.' As in an agony, 'Strive that you may enter in at the strait gate.'"[80] Scripture, prayer, devotional literature, worship, and the Sacraments were too important for Whitefield to abandon. Although Whitefield was fully aware of the differences he had with the Moravians, he nonetheless wrote a cordial letter to Peter Bohler asking forgiveness for mentioning him in his answer to Wesley's sermon "Free Grace." Yet he did not gloss over the problems he had with the Moravians: "I think, my dear brother, you have not acted simply in some things. Let us confess our faults to one another, that we may be healed. I wish there may be no dissention between us for the time to come . . . . I long to have all narrow-spiritedness taken out of my heart."[81] Whitefield had travelled with Bohler through Pennsylvania earlier in 1740, and had referred to him as "a dear lover of the Lord Jesus Christ" and complimented other "German Brethren" for their "order, seriousness, and devotion," and declared them "worthy of imitation."[82] Once again, differences were overlooked in the effort to unite believers who were partakers of experiential religion.

The business dealing that Whitefield engaged in with the Moravians concerned a piece of ground Whitefield purchased "on the forks of the Delaware" river in southeastern Pennsylvania. Whitefield's intent was to construct a house on the property and use it for the education of "negroes." The original tract was composed of five thousand acres, and Whitefield planned on settling "English friends" there on his next trip home. He christened his holding "Nazareth" in 1740. A few miles to the south, the Moravians settled Bethlehem in 1741. Later, unable to continue both the orphan house in Savannah, Georgia, and the "Delaware scheme" in Nazareth, Whitefield transferred ownership of the Pennsylvania property to the Moravians.[83] It was during Zinzendorf's visit to

Pennsylvania that he envisioned the formation of the "Fellowship of God in the Spirit," a "group of committed Christians belonging to various communions who would worship and work together in fellowship with their once crucified, but living Lord and with one another."[84] Since Whitefield had entertained a similar concept, with the Evangelical Revival as the rallying point, it is little wonder that he felt comfortable in a working relationship with the Moravians.

John Wesley owed much to Continental Pietists in general and Moravians in particular. As Ted Campbell points out, Wesley drew inspiration from all strands of Continental Pietism, and reserved a place for Johann Arndt's *True Christianity* in the first volume of his *Christian Library*.[85] Steven O'Malley elaborates on Wesley's Pietistic connection by arguing that the German hymns he chose to translate into English represent his indebtedness to Pietistic expressions of heartfelt worship. One of Wesley's personal favorites was Pietist Gerhard Teersteegen.[86] W.R. Ward has commented:

John Wesley initiated himself into the practical theology of (most every Pietist group) and made no choice among them . . . . If Wesley was to be converted, and the impact of a devotional literature which as a whole had a much heavier soteriological concentration than the Anglicanism in which he had been raised, was that he must be, it was likely that this would happen under Moravian auspices.[87]

Wesley was influenced by Pietistic example as well as by Pietistic writings. He recounted his amazement at Moravians who joyously sang hymns of assurance as a storm threatened to capsize their ship as they journeyed with Wesley to America.[88] He was challenged when questioned by Spangenberg as to whether God's Spirit bore witness with his spirit that "he was a child of God," and mesmerized by his account of the Moravian settlement at Herrnhut.[89] And it was Peter Bohler who encouraged Wesley to "Preach faith till you have it; and then, because you have it, you will preach faith."[90] Wesley also made a pilgrimage to Germany to visit Herrnhut after his Aldersgate experience. But it was a disillusioned Wesley who would soon find in the Moravians theological, liturgical, and personality issues that he could not accept.

Within days of his "warm heart" experience at Aldersgate Street, Wesley embarked on his pilgrimage to Germany. He set out with high hopes, intending to learn from the "holy men who were themselves living witnesses of the full power of faith, and yet able to bear with those that are weak," with the goal of "establishing" his newly found faith on a firm foundation.[91] Initially, he was not disappointed. At Marienborn, he found that for which he searched, ". . . living proofs of the power of faith: Persons saved from inward as well as outward sin, by 'the love of God shed abroad in their hearts;' and from all doubt and fear, by the abiding witness of 'the Holy Ghost given unto them.'"[92] Even after his visit to Herrnhut, he was not disappointed. He wrote of the day of his departure, "O when shall this Christianity cover the earth, as the 'waters cover the sea?'"[93] He continued his *Journal* with accounts of conversations held with notable members of the Moravian community, an outline of the discipline they followed, and an extract of the constitution of the church of the Moravian Brethren.

Nonetheless, Wesley's relationship with the Moravians was beginning to sour. On his trip to Germany, he found many things to commend in the Moravian community:

> What unites my heart to you is, the excellency (in many respects) of the doctrine taught among you: Your laying the true foundation, "God was in Christ, reconciling the world unto himself;" your declaring the free grace of God the cause, and faith the condition, of justification; your bearing witness to those great fruits of faith, "righteousness, and peace, and joy in the Holy Ghost;" and that sure mark thereof, "He that is born of God doth not commit sin."[94]

He also praised them for their love of God, love for each other, their deliverance from outward sin and their excellent discipline. He further approved of their organization and "in general, of (their) great care of the souls committed to (their) charge."[95] The Moravians had a "sincere desire to serve God," but in their sincerity, there lurked hidden dangers.

Wesley was concerned with the lack of community fasting that he found among the Moravians. He believed that Count Zinzendorf was held in too high esteem. Some were not serious enough when it came to spiritual things. The Moravians put their own church on a pedestal, while looking down on those affiliated with other denominations, and did not love their enemies as they should. Wesley was appalled at their use of cunning and secrecy, and their lack of plainness in speaking.[96] He condensed his concerns into a list of three "grand errors" of the Moravians: Universal Salvation, antinomianism, and newly reformed Quietism.[97]

The visible break with the Moravians would not occur until 1740. The Fetter Lane Society, which had been organized on Moravian principles, came under the influence of Moravian P.H. Molther. He taught the Society that one must remain "still" until one received the gift of faith. For Molther, this meant abstaining from all outward means of grace, including prayer, Scripture reading, and the sacraments. To both Charles and John Wesley, this "seemed a denial of the efficacy of the sacraments and other appointed 'means of grace.'"[98] John Wesley wrote in his *Journal* on November 10, 1739, of a woman who actually received the assurance of faith during a celebration of the Lord's Supper. This, for Wesley, was proof against the stillness doctrine. If stillness was the means to receiving assurance of faith, how could one receive it while employing a means of grace? He explains:

1. That there are means of grace, that is, outward ordinances, whereby the inward grace of God is ordinarily conveyed to man; whereby the faith that brings salvation is conveyed to them who before had it not. 2. That one of these means is the Lord's Supper. And, 3. That he who has not this faith ought to wait for it, in the use both of this, and of the other means which God hath ordained.[99]

The actual break was consummated on July 20, 1740, with Wesley withdrawing from the Fetter Lane Society, and setting up another society of like-minded individuals at the Foundery. In leaving Fetter Lane, Wesley cited as the "irreconcilable differences" the Moravian belief that there were no degrees of faith and that no one should use the means of grace until fully assured of saving faith.[100] As with the Quakers, at the heart of Wesley's argument with the Moravians was his contention that the Moravians did not regard Scripture as of primary importance. In writing to his brother Charles, he outlined the reasons why he could not join with the Moravians, chief of which was that their "general scheme is mystical, not scriptural." He concluded this particular letter with a play on the word "assurance" held so dearly by the Moravians, ". . . I will rather, God being my helper, stand quite alone than join with them: I mean till I have full assurance, that they are better acquainted with 'the truth as it is in Jesus.'"[101]

Another major point of contention appeared in direct contact with Count Zinzendorf. A meeting was arranged in September 1741, and the discussion was carried out in Latin, as Wesley's German was as insufficient as Zinzendorf's English. But they understood each other well enough to conflict on the issue of Christian perfection. Zinzendorf argued that, "In the moment he is justified, he is sanctified wholly. From that time he is neither more nor less holy, even unto death . . . . Whenever anyone is justified, the Father, the Son, and the Holy Spirit, dwell in his heart; and from that moment his heart is as pure as it ever will be. A babe in Christ is as pure in heart as a father in Christ. There is no difference." Wesley agreed that there was no difference in the fact of justification of a "babe" and a "father," but sanctification was another story.[102] Wesley had caught a glimpse of the specter of antinomianism lurking in the shadows of Moravianism. If one believed that he or she could become no more holy than at the time of justification, where was the motivation for holy living? The same antinomianism that Wesley detected in the majority of the Church of England and in Calvinism had not allowed Moravianism to slip from its grasp.

But even after the split, Wesley held certain individual Moravians in high regard. As early as August 21, 1740, only one month after leaving the Fetter Lane Society, he spent some time "reflecting how much holier some of them were than me, or any people I had yet known."[103] Obviously, this was well before his interview with Zinzendorf, and it reflected the reality that even though antinomianism was a danger, it was a peril into which not everyone fell.

There was even a sense of "homesickness" that Wesley felt for the fellowship of the Pietistic Moravians. In April 1741, Wesley wrote, "I had a long conversation with Peter Bohler. I marvel how I refrain from joining with these men. I scarce ever see any of them but my heart burns within me. I long to be with them; and yet I am kept from them."[104] The centrality of the Scripture and the vital doctrines of holiness of heart and life were more important to Wesley than the loneliness he sometimes experienced.

Allan Coppedge illustrates that Wesley's dispute with the Moravians is foundational to understanding why he reacted as he did in this and other controversies. The Moravian controversy indicated that there was a clear limit to the latitude Wesley was willing to allow on central doctrines. Wesley also began to see the practical effects of heterodoxy on the spiritual development of believers. Those who accepted the Moravian teaching on stillness stopped using the means of grace. The Moravian debate cemented Wesley's belief in Scripture as the standard for judging theological beliefs. And in confronting antinomianism in Moravians, Wesley became more aware of such tendencies in others, especially Calvinists.[105]

Wesley's relationship with the Moravians was as involved and emotionally draining as his friendship with George Whitefield. The positive Moravian influence on his spiritual development, the fond memories of the Fetter Lane Society, the pilgrimage to Germany, and his friendship with Peter Bohler all added to the difficult decision Wesley felt he had to make in separating from the German Brethren. Yet he never anathematized them nor counted all of them as enemies to Methodist doctrine. In fact, in 1751 in *A Second Letter to the Author of the Enthusiasm of Methodists and Papists Compared*, Wesley reflected on his relationship with the Moravians. Indeed, what he writes about his relationship with Moravians is paradigmatic for his relationship with all he encountered, ". . . I never quarrelled with their persons yet. I did with some of their tenets long ago . . . . I embrace what is good among them, and at the same time reprove what is evil."[106] The evangelical ecumenicity sought by Whitefield and Wesley would consist of no more or no less.

Relations with Roman Catholics

Of all the religious "threats" to the Church of England, none was considered more dangerous than the Roman Catholic Church. The peril it posed was much more than simply a religious issue; at heart, it was an issue of political sovereignty. This fact was evidenced during the English Reformation when centuries-old Praemunire statutes were dusted off and employed to make it illegal for any English citizen to swear allegiance to a foreign power: even if that foreign power happened to be a religious leader, namely, the Pope. In the back of the British national consciousness lurked the ever-present, though rarely evident, menace of Jacobitism. The Jacobite uprising of 1715 may have been somewhat of a distant memory, but the "forty-five" was a present reality in the midst of the Methodist revival.[107] But for all of the differences, the Church of England owed a debt of gratitude to the Catholic Church — a connectedness that Anglicans in the eighteenth century were likely to downplay. Few looked for similarities between members of a Protestant denomination and the Church of Rome unless they were looking for ammunition to fire in an opponent's direction. It is not surprising that the Methodists and evangelicals would have found themselves at great variance with Roman Catholics. That is not to suggest the absence of any similarities or dialogue.[108]

Whitefield's dealings with Roman Catholics were limited to contacts he made on his preaching tours. Unlike Wesley, who was more apt to debate finer points of theology, Whitefield reacted to what he saw and heard. The spectacle of Latin worship was not appealing to him in the least. He was in no way attracted to the spirituality of individual Roman Catholics, but was instead appalled at the superstition he saw attached to their practices. While his ship was docked in Gibraltar in the winter of 1738, he attended the Catholic chapel, only to be flabbergasted at the ornate relics and images of Mary he viewed. He remarked, "Oh! thought I, who hath bewitched this people, that they should thus depart from the simplicity of Christ, and go a whoring after their own inventions? Surely, were the great St. Paul to rise from the dead, and come and view the Romish Church, his spirit would be stirred up within him, as it was at Athens, to see them thus wholly given to idolatry."[109] He attended Mass two weeks later and coolly stated that the most convincing argument against Roman Catholicism was "the pageantry, superstition, and idolatry of their worship."[110]

A sojourn to the Roman stronghold of Ireland further convinced Whitefield of the errors of the Papists. He concluded that the spiritual ignorance of the Catholics of Fourthfargus was because "the key of knowledge is taken from them." The absence of the Scriptures in the vernacular prevented the residents from the opportunity of rescue from the "erroneous principles" of the Roman Catholics. Whitefield was sure that the key to the awakening of the people of Ireland was "to get the Bible translated into their own native language, to have it put in their houses, and (to have) charity schools erected for their children . . . which would insensibly weaken the Romish interest . . ."[111]

The basis of Whitefield's distaste for Roman Catholicism rested on his belief that the Catholic laity were a misguided people. Not only were the Scriptures withheld from them in all their simplicity, but the Catholic clergy acted as cosmic gatekeepers to the entry that led to God's grace. Still in Ireland in November 1738, Whitefield had a conversation with an interested Roman Catholic. He complimented the gentleman for being "more knowing than the generality of those of that persuasion," but quickly ended the admiration by adding that he was "sadly misguided." Whitefield's polemic was gentle, but he attempted to prove that the faithful Roman Catholic was "imposed upon" by the Catholic hierarchy.[112] His argument made an impact, and the gentleman responded that if convinced of this, he would no longer submit to the authority of his priest. Whitefield ended the journal entry by indicating that most of the Protestants and Roman Catholics he met in Ireland placed their faith in their denominational affiliation, while being totally unaware "of inward purity and holiness of heart."[113] Had Whitefield found such understanding among the Roman Catholics he encountered, his relationship with them may have been much warmer. However, no Christian, of Protestant or Roman Catholic loyalties, who was ignorant of experiential religion, was a candidate for cordial fellowship within the Whitefield inner circle.

A visit to Lisbon in 1754 reinforced Whitefield's opinion that Roman Catholicism was little more than superstition, but it was in that visit that Whitefield came as close to finding a positive aspect in Catholicism as he ever would. He witnessed a Passion Week reenactment of the crucifixion and entombment of Jesus. He was disturbed by the superstition and idolatry, but recognized the impression such a presentation could make on an audience. The theatrical Whitefield was not opposed to the use of drama in preaching the gospel. But when the pageantry bred superstition or got in the way of the message, even the "Divine Dramatist" would err on the side of the Gospel.[114]

Stout is likely correct in his assessment of Whitefield and the general Protestant attitude was that he harbored "anti-Catholic sentiments."[115] A notable exception, who attempted to harvest the positive aspects of Latin spirituality from the Church of Rome while discarding the "chaff" of Popery, was John Wesley. Outler and Stout are in agreement when they note that most of the Dissenting bodies of Wesley's time were sure that the Roman Church was not part of the true Church, and was unarguably apostate.[116] In the strict, Church of England definition of the Church, Wesley argued that the majority of the Roman Church was excluded from "the Church catholic," in the universal sense.[117] Still, this did not prevent Wesley from a lifelong study and appreciation of the "warm-hearted" piety that he found in many witnesses from the Latin Church.[118] Ted Campbell argues that the religious climate of all of Europe had produced numerous expressions of experiential spirituality — not simply Protestant, but Catholic, Eastern Orthodox, and even Jewish:

> The religion of the heart movements arose simultaneously . . . among Europeans of widely different confessional traditions who, disgusted with what corporate Christian states had done to each other since the Reformation, and disillusioned with "objective" appeals to scripture and tradition, turned inwardly to a more individualistic and (in a certain sense) "subjective" appropriation of the Christian faith . . . . the extent of John Wesley's borrowing from Puritan, pietistic, and

Catholic devotional literature in his *Christian Library*, demonstrates that these movements were perceived in the eighteenth century as breathing a certain kindred air despite the vast confessional and cultural differences between them.[119]

In spite of the "vast confessional and cultural differences" that were obvious between Wesley and the Roman Catholics he encountered and of whom he wrote, it appears that he believed that what kept Catholics and Protestants apart could be negotiated.[120] Perhaps they were not as far apart as most thought. Whitefield had great difficulty seeing anything positive past the superstitious, idolatrous pageantry he interpreted in the Mass. Wesley dug deeper into the vast holdings of Catholic spirituality and mined the choicest nuggets. Of the two, Wesley displayed the more "Roman Catholic spirit."

Wesley recognized that down through the ages of Church history there had been both "warm hearted" and spiritually "cold" Roman Catholics, just as there had been both in the Church of England camp since the time of the English Reformation. He was deeply impressed by the piety of some Catholics, "Notwithstanding the mixture of superstition which appears in every one of them, yet what a strong vein of piety runs through all! What deep experience of the inward work of God; of righteousness, peace, and joy in the Holy Ghost!"[121] Two decades later he wrote of translating a French tract that would prove helpful for those seeking to be "fervent in spirit." He continued by noting, "How little does God regard men's opinions! What a multitude of wrong opinions are embraced by all the members of the Church of Rome! Yet how highly favored many of them have been!"[122] In his tract *Popery Calmly Considered*, Wesley defended the presence of many "holy men" in Catholic history and the contemporary Church. In spite of their "principles," they had been successful in attaining "holiness of heart and life." He cryptically concluded, however, that, "many of their principles have a natural tendency to undermine holiness."[123] Once again, Wesley felt compelled to warn against the dangers of antinomianism.

Thomas à Kempis and the Marquis de Renty stood as two of Wesley's favorite spiritual guides from the Catholic tradition. Wesley's father had introduced him to à Kempis, and as early as 1725, Wesley viewed him as one who understood the importance of "heart" religion and holiness of life. But he did fault Thomas for being "too strict."[124] Thomas à Kempis' *Imitation of Christ* made a lasting impression on Wesley, and he published several editions of it during his life. Wesley also published an extract of *The Life of Mr. de Renty*. Of this pair he wrote:

But O! that God would write in your hearts the rules of self-denial and love laid down by Thomas a Kempis! Or that you would follow both in this and in good works that burning and shining light of your own church, the Marquis de Renty! Then would all who knew and loved the Lord rejoice to acknowledge you as "the church of the living God."[125]

Such approval of Catholic spirituality raised suspicions in some minds concerning Wesley's loyalties. The republication of Catholic works brought not-unfounded charges of his recommending "popish books." His accuser, Bishop Lavington, noted that Francis de Sales is another "Papist much commended by Mr. Wesley, and who he doubts not is in Abraham's bosom." Wesley pled guilty, "I believe he is in Abraham's bosom."[126] Wesley admitted:

> Whoever they are that have "one Spirit, one hope, one Lord, one faith, one God and Father of all," I can easily bear with their holding wrong opinions, yea, and superstitious modes of worship. Nor would I, on these accounts, scruple still to include them within the pale of the catholic Church.[127]

The assessment that Wesley gave of Roman Catholics is in general much more positive than that of Whitefield. This is not to suggest that Wesley was in complete agreement with the Church of Rome. He had numerous problems with its theology, liturgy, and practice. In a letter to a Roman Catholic priest reproduced in his *Journal*, Wesley outlined the errors he had discovered in Catholicism: seven sacraments, the doctrine of transubstantiation, communion received by the laity in only one kind, purgatory and praying for the release of souls dwelling there, praying to saints, the veneration of relics, the worship of images, the selling of indulgences, the belief in the priority and universality of the Roman Church, and the primacy of the Pope. He found fault in these beliefs because all faithful Catholics "add (these) to those things which are written in the Book of Life." Along with Whitefield, Wesley insisted that "doctrinal development be based in the Scriptures."[128] Wesley further condensed his doctrinal problems with the Catholic Church in *A Word to a Protestant*. In answer to the question, "Why did the Protestant Reformation occur?" Wesley responded by indicating three errors that the Reformers sought to correct: "The making void Christian faith, by holding that man may merit heaven by his own works; the overthrowing the love of God by idolatry; and the (overthrowing) the love of our neighbor by persecution."[129]

On several occasions, Wesley attempted to bridge the chasm between Roman Catholics and Protestants left by the Reformation. He encouraged both sides to mutual understanding and appreciation of the other's view. He made it clear that one's church affiliation did not assure of eternal salvation, ". . . whether you are Protestants or Papists, neither you nor he can ever enter into glory, unless you are now cleansed from all pollution of flesh and spirit, and perfect holiness in the fear of God."[130] Conversely, one's Church affiliation did not automatically exclude one from the possibility of salvation. Here, instead of constantly repeating the differences between the two Churches, Wesley endeavored to find common ground. Specifically, Wesley found two common denominators around which Protestants and Catholics could rally: the worship of God and holy living. He writes in *A Letter to a Roman Catholic*:

> A true Protestant believes in God, has a full confidence in his mercy, fears him with a filial fear, and loves him with all his soul. He worships God in spirit and in truth, in everything gives him thanks; calls upon him with his heart as well as his lips, at all times and in all places; honors his holy name and his word, and serves him truly all the days of his life . . . Now do not you yourself approve of this? Is there any one point you can condemn? Do not you practice as well as approve of it? . . . My dear friend, consider, I am not persuading you to leave or change your religion, but to follow after that fear and love of God without which all religion is vain.[131]

On holy living, Wesley questioned a "reasonable" Catholic as to whether or not they could agree that "profaneness, drunkenness, whoredom, adultery, theft, disobedience to parents, and such like" should be condemned by Christians of whatever persuasion. He proceeded, "And you acknowledge (nay, and frequently for this with a particular earnestness) that every Christian is called to be 'zealous of good works,' as well as to 'deny himself, and take up his cross daily.'"[132] Agreement on these two points would not pull down all walls separating Rome from Canterbury, but could result in "peaceful coexistence:"

> Now, can nothing be done, even allowing us on both sides to retain our own opinions, for the softening of our hearts towards each other, the giving a check to this flood of unkindness, and restoring at least some small degree of love among our neighbors and countrymen? Do not you wish for this? . . . I think you deserve the tenderest regard I can show, were it only because the same God hath raised you and me from the dust of the earth, has made us both capable of loving and enjoying him to eternity; were it only because the Son of God has brought you and me with his own blood. How much more, if you are a person fearing God, (as without question many of you are), and studying to have a conscience void of offence towards God and towards man?[133]

Wesley warmly embraced faith wherever he found it. He found it within the Roman Catholic Church in both ancient and contemporary witnesses. He also understood that many within both Catholic and Protestant Churches stood in need saving faith. In sharing that faith, Wesley found some success among faithful Roman Catholics. He rejoiced in the providence of God that brought him "to the centre of the Papists in Yorkshire," and how this occurred without any forethought on his part.[134]

Other victories won for the Kingdom of God included the case of Michael Parr, once a Catholic, who joined a Methodist Society in Ireland and read his recantation of Catholicism publicly.[135] He told of "a young married woman," a Catholic, who was once very effective at converting "Protestant heretics" to Catholicism, until one day, when several Methodists "converted her" or at least put her on the road to salvation. She was committed to her new pilgrimage, even though her family disowned her, and "desired nothing on earth, but to experience the faith which once she persecuted."[136]

Later that month, he visited a woman who had been a Papist, but had been excommunicated for hearing the Methodists. While praying, she cried and would not be comforted until God "revealed His Son in her heart; which she could not but declare to all that were in the house."[137] Thus, when accused by Bishop Lavington of rejecting "any design to convert others from any communion; and consequently not from popery," Wesley could defend his "catholic spirit," but provide evidence that he had, "by the blessing of God, converted several from popery, who are now alive and ready to testify it."[138] Wesley was willing to accept experiential faith wherever he found it, in whatever denomination in which he found it. But those who wished to make a clean break with their past were more than welcome in the Anglican Methodist fold. Evangelical ecumenicity was still a possibility, even with an evangelical Roman Catholic.

Relations with Calvinists

To say that George Whitefield had generally positive relationships with Calvinists appears to be a masterful statement of the obvious! Conversely, to say that John Wesley typically found himself at loggerheads with Calvinists would fall into the same category of understatement. And while both statements may in essence be valid, it is not fair to the integrity of either man to affirm them in their totality. Whitefield had both warm and adversarial relationships with Calvinists, and Wesley had positive and difficult relationships with Arminians. Likewise, they both had fruitful and strained relationships with those from the other side of the theological aisle. Because Whitefield's personality is so often linked with Calvinistic thought, it is important to examine the relationships both he and Wesley had with those with Calvinistic leanings. These connections provide important insights into the dynamic friendship of Whitefield and Wesley, and offer evidence of the evangelical ecumenicity for which both were striving.[139]

Whitefield nurtured friendships with Calvinists on two continents. From Howell Harris, the Erskines, and Lady Huntingdon in the British Isles to

Jonathan Edwards and the Tennants in North America, Whitefield ministered alongside them and believed their shared Calvinistic theology was the true interpretation of the Scriptures. He wrote in November 1738, "(Jesus Christ) saw me from all eternity; he gave me being; he called me in time; he has freely justified me through faith in his blood; he has in part sanctified me by his spirit; he will preserve me underneath his everlasting arms, till time shall be no more. Oh the blessedness of these evangelical truths! They are indeed gospel."[140] Posted at the same time was a letter to James Hutton, in which Whitefield sang the praises of God's sovereign election and the final perseverance of the saints. "I am persuaded," he wrote, "till a man comes to believe and feel these important truths, he cannot come out of himself; but when convinced of these, and assured of the application of them to his own heart, he then walks by faith indeed, not in himself, but in the Son of God, who died and gave himself for him."[141]

On November 10, 1739, the day these letters were mailed from Philadelphia, Whitefield made the acquaintance of William Tennant, one of the leaders of the First Great Awakening in the colonies, referring to him as "an old grey-headed disciple and soldier of Christ" and as "a great friend of Mr. Erskine, of Scotland."[142] Whitefield would later write to Wesley that the North American revivals were carried on largely through the preaching of those with Calvinistic leanings, and the Tennant family was responsible for a large number of those preachers.[143] Of Jonathan Edwards, another of his North American acquaintances, Whitefield said he is "a solid, excellent Christian" and also preached from his Northampton pulpit.[144] Iain Murray suggests that these contacts with the Tennants and Edwards in 1740 helped cement his Calvinistic theology, as he could see the pragmatic results of their preaching.[145]

More germane to a study of eighteenth-century British Methodism, however, are the relationships that Whitefield cultivated with Calvinists on the other side of the Atlantic. Two such relationships are especially telling. His relationship with Howell Harris is important, as he was a convinced Calvinist and because of his later attempts at healing the rift between Wesley and the Calvinists. His relationship with the Erskines in Scotland is also illuminating, as it showed that Whitefield could disagree with Calvinists as well.

Howell Harris was the leading figure of the evangelical revival in Wales during the time of the Wesleys and Whitefield. Harris had been preaching in the fields of Wales for several years before Whitefield adopted the practice. Stout notes that as early as December of 1738, Whitefield began corresponding with Harris in admiration of his evangelistic successes.[146] Thus began a friendship that would last through their lifetimes, although they spent little time together. Only a month after the initial correspondence, Whitefield wrote excitedly to another, "Mr. Howell Harris, and I, are correspondents, blessed by God! May I follow him, as he does Jesus Christ."[147] Harris and Whitefield met in March 1739, as Whitefield made a short preaching tour of Wales. As a result of that meeting, Whitefield described Harris as having a catholic spirit; one "who loves all who love our Lord Jesus Christ."[148] It was a character that Whitefield valued in other people and prided in possessing himself. The magnanimous, catholic spirited Harris would be instrumental in repairing the breach between Wesley and Whitefield.

Whitefield soon departed for America. He wrote to Harris twice during the course of his trans-Atlantic crossing. The first letter simply related Whitefield's desire to return to Wales for another preaching tour. But in the second letter, he pointed out to Harris the affinities between them: "Our principles agree, as face answers face in the water. Since I saw you, God has been pleased to enlighten me more in that comfortable doctrine of Election, &c. At my return, I hope to be more explicit than I have been. God forbid, my dear brother, that we should shun to declare the whole counsel of God."[149]

Prior to meeting the Tennants and Edwards, Whitefield was becoming more and more convinced of the truth of Calvinism. It is also clear that Wesley's decision to "preach and print" his sermon *Free Grace* was accompanied simultaneously by Whitefield's decision "to be more explicit" in his pronouncement of "the decrees." To blame one or the other for "casting the first stone" is unfair to both. Each one came to their decisions independent of each other, and, conveniently, while separated by the Atlantic!

It is not surprising that Whitefield's letters to Harris were replete with references to their commitment to Calvinistic theology, but also revealed a Whitefield concerned for those who had fallen into the "snare" of Arminianism and for the state of his friendship with Wesley. He wrote to Harris from Savannah on February 4, 1740, "Oh the free-grace of Christ Jesus our Lord! . . . Let us continually preach up free-grace, though we die for it; we cannot lose our lives in a better cause . . . . Methinks I hear you say, 'Glory be to free grace: All praise be given to electing love.' Let all that love the Lord Jesus say, Amen!"[150] He wrote again on September 24, 1740, sharing his concerns over the problems in the Fetter Lane Society, noting that he feared the members were "running into sad errors." He also referenced a meeting Harris had with Wesley, hoping that their conversation was "blessed." Of Wesley, Whitefield prays, "O that the Lord may batter down his free-will, and complete him to own his sovereignty and everlasting love . . . . O that all would study the covenant of grace! The more I look into it, the more is my soul delighted."[151]

Elsewhere, Whitefield responded to questions Harris had concerning Christian perfection, good works, and the Christian's assurance of salvation. Whitefield counseled:

We shall never have such a dominion over indwelling sin, as entirely to be delivered from the stirring of it . . . . It is equally true, that we shall not rest wholly from working for life. For whilst there is any part of us unregenerate, that part will be always leading us to the old covenants . .

. . As for assurance, I cannot but think, all who are truly converted must know that there was a time in which they closed with Christ: But then, as so many have died only with an humble hope, and have been even under doubts and fears, though they could not but be looked upon as Christians; I am less positive than once I was, lest haply I should condemn some of God's dear children.[152]

Aside from Whitefield and Harris' collegial correspondence on points of Calvinistic doctrine, and sharing of concerns over Arminianism, perhaps the most poignant of Whitefield's letters are those he wrote to Harris on the differences that arose with the Scottish Presbyterians. He spent three months in Scotland in the late summer of 1741, his preaching accompanied by its usual triumphs. Yet on August 13, he wrote to Harris:

I utterly disapprove of some persons' separating principles. I find, Satan now turns himself into an angel of light, and stirs up God's children to tempt me to come over to some particular party. The associate Presbytery have been hard upon me; but I find no freedom any longer than I continue just as I am, and evangelize to all. I know not that I differ from you in one thing.[153]

En route to Scotland for a second preaching tour, Whitefield was here writing with a sense of high expectation.[154] Other letters written during his stay revealed that his expectations became reality, with numerous preaching opportunities marked by multitudes of conversions. But on August 26, 1742, Whitefield wrote to Harris from Cambuslang, the epicenter of revival in Wales:

The glorious Redeemer seems to be advancing from congregation to congregation, carrying all before him. The Messrs, E.'s people have kept a fast for me, and give out, that all the work now in Scotland is only delusion, and by the agency of the devil. O, my dear brother, to what great lengths in bigotry and prejudice may good men run? Blessed be God, I can see the differences between God's children, and yet love them from my heart.[155]

At a first glance is seems strange that Whitefield should have difficulties with others whose views were so similar to his own. But the disagreement with the Erskines concerned ecclesiology more than Calvinistic theology. The Erskine brothers, Ralph and Ebenezer, had been ordained by the Scottish Kirk, but had withdrawn in order to form a separatist "Associate Presbytery." Stout describes them as "militantly Calvinistic in theology and jealously protective of their lay prerogatives. They opposed the 'tyranny' of presbyteries and synods and insisted that each congregation be free to choose and ordain its own pastor."[156] Whitefield had no trouble with the "militant Calvinism," but supporting the Associate Presbytery in its separation from the Church posed another problem.

Whitefield never deemed necessary a separation from the Church of England. He successfully defended his Calvinistic principles throughout his lifetime as a member of the Anglican clergy. Thus the Erskines' hybrid of separatist Calvinism was much less attractive to Whitefield than the more "evangelically ecumenical" Calvinism he was attracted to in Edwards and Tennant.[157]

Whitefield wrote to Ralph Erskine on subjects ranging from Calvinistic theology to marital advice. On November 28, 1739, he wrote praising Erskine as one of several "burning and shining lights to appear . . . in this midnight of the church." He went on to highlight the kinship he had with Erskine:

> I bless God, his spirit has convinced me of our eternal election by the Father through the Son, of our free justification through faith in his blood, of our sanctification as the consequence of that, and of our final perseverance and glorification as the result of all. These I am persuaded God has joined together; these, neither men nor devils shall ever be able to put asunder.[158]

Yet within a few months, Whitefield became concerned over the separatist tendencies the Associate Presbytery espoused. Whitefield objects to their insisting exclusively on the presbyterian form of government, cautioning that such a stance would lead the Erskines to "persecute all that differ . . . in their church government, or outward way of worshipping God." He had consulted the more moderate Gilbert Tennant, who promised to write to Erskine regarding his views. "As for my own part," continued Whitefield, "(though I profess myself a minister of the church of England) I am of a catholic spirit; and if I see a man who loves the Lord Jesus in sincerity, I am not very solicitous to what outward communion he belongs. The kingdom of God, I think, does not consist in any such thing."[159] When encouraged by Ralph Erskine to join the Associate Presbytery, Whitefield wrote to Ralph's brother Ebenezer, informing him that he had concluded that it was unnecessary:

> I come only as an occasional preacher, to preach the simple gospel to all that are willing to hear me, of whatever denomination. It will be wrong in me to join in a reformation as to church government, any further than I have light given me from above. If I am quite neuter as to that in my preaching, I cannot see how it can hinder or retard any design you may have on foot. My business seems to be, to evangelize, to be a Presbyter at large . . . . I write this, that there may not be the least misunderstanding between us. I love and honor the associate

Presbytery in the bowels of Jesus Christ . . . . But let them not be offended, if in all things I cannot immediately fall in with them.[160]

Echoing this theme, Whitefield wrote to Ralph Erskine on June 4, 1741, that he felt the Associate Presbytery was being "too hard" on him. "I come simply to preach the gospel, and to be received only as an occasional itinerant preacher by all, and not to enter into any particular connection whatever."[161] In these two letters, Whitefield illustrated his determination to unite believers under the banner of the revival, not under any particular denomination. However, their differences led to an open breach. Whitefield wrote to Ebenezer Erskine on June 10, 1742:

It is some concern to me, that our difference as to outward things, should cut off our sweet fellowship and communion with each other. God knows my heart, I highly value and honour you . . . I applaud your zeal for God; and though, in some respects, I think it not according to knowledge, and to be levelled frequently against me, yet indeed I feel no resentment in my heart, and should joyfully sit down and hear you and your other brethren preach . . . . O when shall the time come, when the watchmen will see eye to eye? Hasten the time, our Lord and our God![162]

The catholic-spirited Grand Itinerant was willing to preach the gospel of God's free grace wherever he found an audience. He would not allow anyone, not even like-minded Calvinists, to prevent him from fulfilling his divine commission. Those who tried to limit the scope of his itinerations were working against him, not with him. To Whitefield, "the Word of God was not bound," and neither was the revival.[163]

Wesley's disputes with Calvinistic evangelicals are not nearly as surprising as Whitefield's. By virtue of his belief in the unlimited atonement, Christian perfection, and the possibility of a believer falling from grace, he was naturally set at odds with those of the Calvinist persuasion. But these differences did not prevent him from carrying on fruitful dialogue with defenders of "the divine decrees." Indeed, Wesley was not adverse to employing John Calvin himself, when he served his purposes. He referred to Calvin as "a great instrument of God" and "a wise and pious man," even though his treatment of Michael Servetus tainted Wesley's image of him.[164] On another occasion, Wesley was confronted with the argument that many of his Methodist preachers were not ordained. He replied, ". . . was Mr. Calvin ordained? Was he either a priest or deacon?"[165] In spite of the Servetus affair, Wesley still thought enough of Calvin to help him prove a point.

Wesley and the Arminian Methodists were regularly charged with denying original sin and justification by faith. Wesley pled "not guilty" to both charges:

No man that ever lived, not John Calvin himself, ever asserted either original sin, or justification by faith, in more strong, more clear and express terms, than Arminius has done. These two points, therefore, are to be set out of the question: In these both parties agree. In this respect, there is not a hair's breadth difference between Mr. Wesley and Mr. Whitefield.[166]

Wesley's catholic spirit extended to accusative Calvinists. He encouraged both Calvinists and Arminians to avoid using such terms in a perjorative sense, and stated that preachers on both sides should lead by example.[167]

Even in the beloved Fetter Lane Society, already distressed by the Moravian controversy, Calvinism entered into the debate. A member of the society, Mr. Arcourt, held to the belief in double predestination, but was welcome to continue in the Society if those of his opinion would "not trouble others by disputing about it." Arcourt responded that he would continue the dispute at every opportunity, as Wesley and others were "all wrong" and he planned to set them "all right." The following day, Wesley told the society of Arcourt's plan of spreading to "all the world" that John and Charles were "false prophets." John Wesley concluded, ". . . without entering into the controversy, (1) I besought all of them who were weak in the faith, not to 'receive one another to doubtful disputations;' but simply to follow after holiness, and the things that make for peace."[168] Wesley was content to call Presbyterians and Independents "my brethren," as they were "at the smallest distance from us."[169] For Wesley as for Whitefield, the most basic question was:

Have you received the Holy Ghost? . . . . Without which (that) you confess outward religion, whether negative or positive, is nothing . . . . Beware you never account yourself a Christian, no, not in the lowest degree, till God hath sent forth the Spirit of Christ into your heart, and that Spirit bear witness with your spirit, that you are a child of God.[170]

Not all of Wesley's dealings with Calvinists were in as gentle a spirit. There were theological differences, and at times they needed to be addressed in the strongest possible terms. Just as he saw the danger of antinomianism lurking in Moravianism, he sensed its presence in Calvinism as well. The holiness of heart and life was instrumental to Methodism, and anything that endangered that had to be confronted. Wesley reflected:

In 1737, (two young men) saw holiness comes by faith. They saw likewise, that men are justified before they are sanctified; but still holiness was their point. God then thrust them out, utterly against their will, to raise a holy people. When Satan could no otherwise hinder this, he threw Calvinism in the way; and then Antinomianism, which strikes directly at the root of all holiness.[171]

Regarding Christian perfection, Wesley reported, "The Calvinists say . . . it will be attained as soon as the soul and body part."[172] Wesley believed that such a doctrine was the "direct antidote" to the doctrine of "heart-holiness," as it provided no motivation for holy living. In fact, it provided an excuse for giving up in the pursuit of holiness. Of "all the devices of Satan . . . for stopping the work of God," Calvinism was viewed by Wesley as the greatest danger to the *grand depositum* of the Methodists. He suggested that the best ways to guard against the inherent dangers of Calvinism were for all Methodist preachers to read Fletcher's tracts, preach in a loving, non-controversial way, and "mildly expose" the Calvinists when "time served." They were also to "guard the tender minds" of new converts against Calvinism; answer all objections in public and private; advise Methodists not to hear them; and pray that "God would stop the plague."[173] The peril lay in the fact that "the truth of the Gospel . . . lies within a hair's breadth" of both Calvinism and antinomianism. The Methodist interpretation of "Gospel truth" came close to Calvinism by "ascribing all good to the free grace of God," by denying the possibility of an unaided human response to God's grace, and by denying any human merit in salvation. Methodism's proximity to antinomianism was evident in that both "exalt the merits of Christ," while downplaying human potential, and by encouraging "rejoicing evermore" in Christ's merits.[174]

Wesley's assessment of Calvinism may have been generally negative, but his estimation of certain Calvinists could be more positive. Aside from his friendship with Whitefield, Wesley's relationship with Howell Harris included many of the same characteristics of evangelical ecumenicity. As early as June 1739, Harris had been encouraged to steer clear of Wesley's preaching, as it was tainted with Arminianism. But upon hearing him preach, Harris said, "I quickly found what spirit you was of. And before you had done, I was so over-powered with joy and love, that I had much ado to walk home."[175] The impression upon Harris was so great that he invited Wesley to come to Wales. During his preaching tour, Harris confided in Wesley that many had tried to prejudice him against the visiting Arminian. Their attempts were in vain, and Wesley intoned, "And yet these are good Christians."[176]

Even Wesley's visible separation from Whitefield did little to quench Harris' catholic spirit. On a subsequent trip to Wales in October 1741, Wesley referred to him as, "Thou man of peace," who still willingly employed him in Wales, albeit of different theology. On October 17, Harris encouraged several ardent Calvinists, bent on sparring with Wesley on theological issues, "to follow after the things that make for peace; and God blessed the healing words which he spoke; so that we parted in much love, being all determined to let controversy alone, and to preach 'Jesus Christ, and him crucified.'"[177]

Wesley reciprocated with a similar spirit during the course of their friendship. He wrote to Harris on August 6, 1742:

> And what is it that we contend about? Allow such a perfection as you have there described (in your letter), and all further dispute I account vain jangling and mere strife of words. As to the other point, we agree, 1. That no man can have any power except it be given him from above. 2. That no man can merit anything but hell, seeing all other merit is in the blood of the Lamb. For those two fundamental points, both you and I earnestly contend. Why then, if we both disclaim all power and all merit in man, what need of this great gulf to be fixed between us? Brother, is thy heart with mine, as my heart is with thy heart? If it be, give me thy hand . . . . so long as I am continued in the work, let us rise up together against the evil doers . . . . The good Lord blot out all that is past, and let there henceforward be peace between me and thee![178]

Harris responded:

> I see that little by little the Lord will bring us together. We have been perhaps in your eyes too far leaning towards Reprobation, though we never meant it in the least, as to set man's damnation on God's decretive willing it unconditionally. We try to secure God's glory in man's salvation; and you try to secure His Justice by setting man's damnation in his own will. It is probably the duty of all of us to be more careful with our words.[179]

However, Harris would not merely be "there" for Wesley during the early Calvinistic controversy with Whitefield. Both prior to and after the major Calvinistic controversy that came to a head after Whitefield's death in 1770, Harris again played his peacekeeping role. Wesley noted that on Thursday, August 20 and Friday, August 21, 1767, he met with many Methodist stewards and local preachers, along with Whitefield and Harris. Wesley commented, "Love and harmony reigned from the beginning to the end; but we have all need of more love and holiness; and, in order thereto, of crying continually, 'Lord, increase our faith!'"[180] In the wake of the ensuing controversy, Harris invited Wesley to preach at Trevecka, and of their meeting Wesley said, ". . . and we found our hearts knit together as at the beginning."[181]

The Paradigm Takes Shape

The abundant evidence strongly suggests that both George Whitefield and John Wesley were endeavoring to build a consensus among Christian believers of all denominations. Whitefield carried on cordial relationships with individuals from backgrounds far different from his own — not only with Quakers and German Moravians, but also with Lutherans and even Deists![182] Conversely, some with whom he should have been closest doctrinally, were most at odds with him ecclesiastically. The situation was much the same with Wesley's personal relationships. His range of acquaintances was broad; from Calvinists like Whitefield and Harris to Roman Catholics to whom he wrote irenic pleas for understanding. By the same token, those with whom he should have been closest, namely the Moravians, who were so instrumental in his personal spiritual development, exchanged some of his most heated vitriol. Thus, it is completely inadequate to suggest that Whitefield and Wesley split simply over differences in theology. Both "split" with groups who were in much closer doctrinal agreement than they were, and both carried on relationships with those who were in great theological disagreement with them. What clearly appears is that Whitefield and Wesley were in search of evangelical ecumenicity, a consensus of "warm-hearted" believers from the great traditions of Roman Catholicism, evangelicalism, and the Reformed faith.[183] Both claimed to possess a "catholic spirit" that had a broad enough bottom to encompass all believers who sought holiness of heart and life. As Gabriel Fackre has pointed out in a contemporary context, "catholicity," "ecumenicity," and "evangelical" are not mutually exclusive terms. Evangelicals described as possessing a "catholic spirit" were those who accepted Scripture as the source of authority, with the Church, "the whole people of God," as the resource for interpreting the Scripture, and "general human experience — rational, moral, affective" — constituting "the setting in which one reads Scripture and tradition."[184]

Whitefield and Wesley's shared emphases on Scripture, tradition, and experiential Christianity formed the heart of their evangelical ecumenicity. With Whitefield attempting to unite Christians from all denominations under the banner of the revival, and Wesley's leadership in cultivating the "revived" into the Methodist classes, all the ingredients for success in building an evangelical consensus were present. Yet for a time, Whitefield and Wesley found it necessary to separate for what appear, on the surface, to be theological differences. Other reasons, more directly involved in the breach, were present. They would be overcome, and George Whitefield and John Wesley would bequeath to the Church the blueprint for future proponents of evangelical ecumenicity who would seek to unite all who believe religion must be lived experientially.

Notes

1. Allan Coppedge, *John Wesley in Theological Debate* (Wilmore, KY: Wesley Heritage Press, 1987), 118. He also suggests that the Thirty-Nine Articles played a part in framing Wesley's "Catholic Spirit." But since Wesley believed the Articles to be derived from Scripture, this is not surprising. See Coppedge, 172-174.

2. Whitefield, *Journals*, 69.

3. Ibid., 90.

4. Ibid., 249-250.

5. Ibid., 259.

6. Whitefield, *Letters*, 49. Letter XLVI to James Hervey at Dummer.

7. Whitefield, *Journals*, 348.

8. Ibid., 286.

9. Ibid., 256.

10. Ibid., 256.

11. Ibid., 258.

12. Whitefield, *Letters*, 93-94. Letter XCVIII, written November 10, 1739. The editors add that this letter was written to a Church of England clergyman "not of the Methodist persuasion."

13. Ronald Knox, *Enthusiasm: A Chapter in the History of Religion with Special Reference to the Seventeenth and Eighteenth Centuries* (New York: Oxford University Press, 1961), 506.

14. Although somewhat dated, Knox's work gives a more negative Roman Catholic assessment of Wesley than Piette did earlier in the century. Knox suggests that Wesley was the cause of strained relations due to his habit of seeking a preaching place in a local church, and when rebuffed, preaching in another place within the parish. Knox notes that parish clergy were well within their rights to refuse their pulpit even to another clergyman of the established Church. Knox, 506.

15. Outler, ed., *John Wesley*, 122.

16 Ibid., 125. Wesley is quoting from the homily "Of the Salvation of Mankind."

17. Ibid., 126-127. From the homily "Salvation."

18. Henry D. Rack, *Reasonable Enthusiast: John Wesley and the Rise of Methodism* (Nashville: Abingdon Press, 1992), 305.

19. Rupert Davies, ed., *The Works of John Wesley, Vol. 9: The Methodist Societies, History, Nature, and Design* (Nashville: Abingdon, 1989), 334.

20. Ibid., 336.

21. Cragg, 313.

22. Ibid., 82-83.

23. Ibid., 76.

24. Rack, 293.

25. Cragg, 115. From *A Farther Appeal to Men of Reason and Religion, Part I.*

26. Ibid., 78.

27. Ibid., 75-76.

28. Ibid., 73.

29. Ibid., 321.

30. Rupert E. Davies, ed., *The Methodist Societies: History, Nature, and Design, Vol. 9* (Nashville: Abingdon, 1989), 339. Quoted in *Reasons Against A Separation from the Church of England.*

31. John Wesley, *Works, Vol XIII*, 34. Letter DCXII, penned October 18, 1778.

32. Ibid., 304.

33. Cragg, 185.

34. Indeed, there was one key area of disagreement between Whitefield and the Society of Friends: the issue of slavery. While Whitefield was a slave owner and has been credited with being a major player in influencing the colony of Georgia to legalize slavery, he was also committed to preaching the gospel to African Americans, fully believing that certain of them were part of God's elect. William Sloat II argues that Whitefield's promotion of slavery was consistent with his belief that America provided ample opportunity for African Americans to respond to the gospel, and that he saw it as an important aspect of his social ministry to encourage humane treatment of slaves. Sloat concludes, "To Whitefield, the answer to the injustice faced by African American slaves, did not lie in an attack on the institution of slavery, but in the conversion of the master and the slave. Whitefield was one of many in his day who saw regeneration of all of the people of the world as both essential and possible. His treatment of African Americans fit those two convictions: the two convictions to which he gave his whole life." William Sloat II, "George Whitefield, African-Americans, and Slavery," *Methodist History* 33 (1994): 3-13.

35. Whitefield, *Journals*, 237.

36. Ibid., 271.

37. Ibid., 236.

38. Ibid., 240.

39. Ibid., 304.

40. Ibid., 312.

41. Ibid., 362.

42. Ibid., 406. Whitefield lodged in Wilmington on his way to Chester and Philadelphia. The circumstances suggest that the same individuals provided hospitality to Whitefield on these two occasions. Whitefield neglects to list the names of his hosts on these two trips.

43. Ibid., 498.

44. Whitefield, *Letters*, 79. The letter is numbered LXXXII, and is addressed to, "Rev. and Dear Sir," dated November 10, 1739.

45. Ibid., 504. The letter is numbered as Letter 21 in the Banner of Truth edition of Whitefield's letters.

46. Ibid., 507-508. Letter 25. This is not to suggest that Whitefield felt this way about all Quakers. Indeed, Whitefield had indicated that many Quakers were not self-righteous nor bigoted, as many had been very hospitable toward him. He appears to be referring to a limited number of Quaker leaders, perhaps even civic leaders. His addressing this letter to "a friend" should not be misconstrued to indicate that Whitefield was writing to a member of the Society of Friends.

47. Whitefield, *Journals*, 237.

48. Ibid., 234.

49. Ibid., 335.

50. Ibid., 341. Far from advocating justification by works, Whitefield is emphasizing that the imputed righteousness of Christ in the believer will overflow into good works. Accusations that Whitefield was an antinomian were unfounded.

51. Ibid., 387.

52. Ibid., 313. The letter was dated July 21, 1739.

53. Ibid., 252.

54. Ibid., 265. The first occasion was on Wednesday, May 16, the latter on June 2. Stonehouse was a priest in Islington. It was to Stonehouse that Whitefield wrote, "And is one of the priests also obedient to the word? Blessed be God, the Father of our Lord Jesus Christ, who hath translated you from darkness to light; from the power of Satan to the service of the ever-living God . . . . Glory be to his free grace that you are one of the happy number." Whitefield, *Letters*, 192-193. The letter is number CCII, and is dated June 26, 1740. Whitefield wrote from Savannah, Georgia.

55. John Wesley, *Works, Vol. X*, 177. The letter is titled, *A Letter to a Person Lately Joined with the People Called Quakers*.

56. Ibid., 178.

57. Ibid., 178.

58. Ibid., 178.

59. Ibid., 178.

60. Ibid., 182-183.

61. Ibid., 183. Wesley notes the Scriptural argument Barclay proposes for the doctrine of silence. Psalm 27:14, "Wait on the Lord: Be of good courage, and he shall strengthen thine heart;" Psalm 37:7, 34, "Rest in the Lord, and wait patiently; fret not thyself at him who prospereth his way . . . Wait on the Lord, and keep his way, and he shall exalt thee to inherit the land;" Proverbs 20:22, "Say not thou, I will recompense evil; but wait on the Lord and he shall save thee." Barclay's prooftexts are pretexts as far as Wesley is concerned.

62. Ibid., 184-185. The debate over stillness would occupy Wesley in his ongoing debate with the Moravian brothers and sisters. It is addressed in more detail below, in the section on Wesley's relationship with the Moravians.

63. Frank Baker, ed., *Letters of John Wesley, Vol. 26* (Oxford: Clarendon Press, 1982), 203.

64. Ward and Heitzenrater, *Journal and Diaries, Vol. 19* (Nashville: Abingdon, 1990), 53.

65. Ibid., 88. According to Ward and Heitzenrater, this individual may have been Thomas Whitehead.

66. Ibid., 141.

67. Ibid., 341.

68. Ward and Heitzenrater, *Journal and Diaries, Vol. 20*, 129. The *Appeal* the Quaker refers to is probably *A Farther Appeal to Men of Reason and Religion, Parts II and III*, the first edition of which was published in London by Strahan in 1745. Third and fourth editions followed in 1746; a second edition has yet to be found. See Cragg, 549. In *Parts II and III*, Wesley has some strong words for Quakers. While they claimed to have been sent to reform the Church, Wesley said their "open, avowed, total separation from the Church and their vehement invectives against many of her doctrines" belied the fact that they were more concerned about "opinions and externals rather than in preaching about faith, mercy, and the love of God." Cragg, 319. He also questioned whether Quakers truly understood the nature of saving faith (Cragg, 259) and "the inward principle" that they were so fond of defending (Cragg, 258).

69. Ward and Heitzenrater., *Vol. 21*, 49.

70. Ibid., *Vol. 20*, 283.

71. Wesley recorded baptizing seven who were "educated among the Quakers" on April 6, 1748 (Ward and Heitzenrater, *Vol. 20*, 217); three more on August 2, 1752 (Ibid., 435); Elizabeth Kershaw, "late a Quaker," on May 1, 1747 (Ibid., 170); three individuals on April 29 and 30, 1750 (Ibid., 334); and Hannah C., on October 16, 1756 (Ibid., *Vol. 21*, 79).

72. Whitefield, *Journals*, 386-387.

73. Leon O. Hynson, "Wesley's *Thoughts upon Slavery*: A Declaration of Human Rights," *Methodist History* 33 (1994): 46. Blackstone's *Commentaries on the Laws of England* were not only instrumental in the British legal system, but found expression in America's courts also. Also helpful to understanding Wesley's ethics as they relate to slavery and, with with Quakers, is: Leon O. Hynson, *To Reform the Nation: Theological Foundations of Wesley's Ethics* (Grand Rapids: Francis Asbury Press, 1984), 142-147.

74. Frank Baker, "The Origins, Character, and Influence of John Wesley's *Thoughts upon Slavery*," *Methodist History* 22 (1984): 77. Benezet published: *Observations on the Enslaving, Importing, and Purchasing of Negroes* (Germantown, 1759); *A Short Account of that Part of Africa, inhabited by the Negroes* (Philadelphia, 1762); *A Caution and Warning to Great Britain and her Colonies, in a short Representation of the calamitous State of the enslaved Negroes in the British Dominions* (Philadelphia, 1766); and *Some Historical Account of Guinea, its situation, produce, and the general disposition of its inhabitants. With an inquiry into the rise and progress of the slave trade, its nature, and lamentable effects. Also, a re-publication of the Sentiments of several Authors of Note, on this interesting Subject; particularly an Extract of a Treatise, by Granville Sharp.*

75. Hynson, *Wesley's 'Thoughts upon Slavery*, 49. Baker calculated the number at around 30%. Baker, "Origins, Character, and Influence of . . . *Thoughts upon Slavery*," 79.

76. Wesley, *Works, Vol. X*, 187. From *A Letter to a Person lately joined with the people called Quakers.*

77. The classic work on Wesley's relationship with the Moravian Church is: Clifford W. Towlson, *Moravian and Methodist: Relationships and Influences in the Eighteenth Century* (London: Epworth Press, 1957). A concise, helpful analysis is: Leon O. Hynson, "John Wesley and the *Unitas Fratrum*: A Theological Analysis," *Methodist History* 18 (1979): 26-60. Methodist/Moravian relations are further explored in: F. Ernest Stoeffler, "Religious Roots of the Early Moravian and Methodist Movements," *Methodist History* 24 (1986): 132-140; Warren Thomas Smith, "Eighteenth Century Encounters: Methodist-Moravian," *Methodist History* 24 (1986): 141-156; and Kenneth E. Rowe, "From Eighteenth Century Encounter to Nineteenth Century Estrangement: Images of Moravians in the Thought of Methodist Bishops Asbury and Simpson," *Methodist History* 24 (1986): 171-178.

78. Whitefield, *Letters*, 441. Letter CCCCLVII, dated September 24, 1742.

79. Whitefield, *Journals*, 459. Wesley withdrew from the Fetter Lane Society, largely over this issue, only two months before Whitefield made this journal entry on September 20, 1740.

80. Whitefield, *Letters*, 228. From letter CCXL, dated December 11, 1740. Apparently, this letter was written to a member of the Fetter Lane Society who had accepted the Moravian teaching of "stillness," abstaining from all usage of the means of grace.

81. Ibid., 332. Letter CCCLXIV, dated October 10, 1741. In his response to Wesley's "Free Grace," Whitefield accused Bohler of holding to the doctrine of universal salvation to such an extent that "all the damned souls would hereafter be brought out of hell." See Whitefield. *Journals*, 587.

82. Whitefield, *Journals*, 412.

83. Ibid., 411. The Whitefield House in Nazareth has served the Moravian Church over the years in numerous ways. Currently it is home to the Moravian Historical Society.

84. Stoeffler, 132.

85. Ted A. Campbell, *The Religion of the Heart: A Study of European Religious Life in the Seventeenth and Eighteenth Centuries* (Columbia, SC: University of South Carolina Press, 1991), 124. Wesley's *Christian Library* was a collection of the best devotional literature in the history of Christianity up to Wesley's day. Always an avid borrower of material, Wesley abridged and edited the selections he judged worthy of inclusion.

86. J. Steven O'Malley, "Pietistic Influence on John Wesley: Wesley and Gerhard Tersteegen," *Wesleyan Theological Journal*, 31(1996): 50. O'Malley highlights the affinities between Tersteegen and Wesley, "Both had a singular devotion to encouraging the operation of saving grace in the lives of the spiritually lost of all levels of society; both maintained an itinerant ministry of evangelism, coupled with organizing discipleship groups; both were gifted in hymnody, and both had a non-sectarian attitude toward their respective state churches," 57.

87. W.R. Ward. *The Protestant Evangelical Awakening* (New York: Cambridge University Press, 1992), 311.

88. Ward and Heitzenrater, *Journal and Diaries, Vol. 19*, 143.

89. Ibid., 146.

90. Ibid., 228. The Fetter Lane Society was set up on principles suggested by Peter Bohler; see entry for May 1, 1738.

91. Ibid., 254.

92. Ibid., 260.

93. Ibid., 272.

94. Ward and Heitzenrater, *Journal and Diaries, Vol. 19*, 117.

95. Ibid., 221.

96. Ibid., 221.

97. Ibid., 222.

98. Campbell, 125.

99. Ibid., 121.

100. Ibid., 162.

101. Ibid., 191.

102. Ibid., 213-214.

103. Ibid., 165.

104. Ibid., 190.

105. Coppedge, 62.

106. Cragg, 413.

107. The uprisings of 1715 and 1745 are treated above, on pages 9 - 11, as they relate to setting the political context of this study. It is interesting to note, that during "the Forty-Five," it was rumored that Wesley had spent time in France and Spain, was a protege of the Pretender, and that he was forming "Methodist" societies to assist in a Catholic *coup d'etat*. Ward and Heitzenrater, *Journal and Diaries, Vol. 20*, 78.

108. Wesley's relationship with Roman Catholics has been outlined in: John M. Todd. *John Wesley and the Catholic Church* (London: Hodder and Stoughton, 1958) and in cursory form by Outler in his one-volume abridgment of Wesley's theology (Oxford, 1964). See also: Aelred Burrows, "Wesley the Catholic," in *John Wesley: Contemporary Perspectives*, ed. John Stacey (London: Epworth Press, 1988), 54-66.

109. Whitefield, *Journals*, 128.

110. Ibid., 136.

111. Ibid., 181.

112. Whitefield employed this argument on at least one other occasion. On Sunday, November 11, 1739, after speaking out against the "unchristian principles and practices of our clergy," and noting that he attempts to do this in the right spirit, he notes, "Were I to convert Papists, my business would be to shew that they were misguided by their priests; and if I want to convince Church of England Protestants, I must prove that the generality of their teachers do not preach or live up to the truth as it is in Jesus. In vain do we hope to set people right till we demonstrate that the way which they have been taught is wrong." Ibid., 346.

113. Ibid., 183.

114. Stout, 217. It is also in Lisbon that Whitefield sees a disturbing window depicting the Spanish Inquisition, complete with representations of decapitated Jewish "heretics." While the window is a part of Roman Catholic history, Whitefield is astonished at the message it "preaches." The "gospel" preached is one of fear, not of the free, saving mercy of Jesus Christ.

115. Ibid., 57.

116. Outler, *John Wesley,* 351.

117. Ibid., 313.

118. Ibid., 351.

119. Campbell, 177.

120. Outler, *John Wesley,* 351.

121. Ward and Heitzenrater, *Journal and Diaries, Vol. 20,* 200.

122. Ibid., *Vol. 22,* 199-120.

123. John Wesley, *Works, Vol. X* (Peabody: Hendrickson, 1991), 155.

124. Ward and Heitzenrater, *Journal and Diaries, Vol. 18,* 243.

125. Cragg, 261. From *A Farther Appeal to Men of Reason and Religion, Part II.*

126. Ibid., 426. From *A Second Letter to the Author of the Enthusiasm of Methodists and Papists Compared.*

127. Outler, *John Wesley,* 314.

128. Ward and Heitzenrater, *Journal and Diaries, Vol. 19,* 92.

129. John Wesley, *Works, Vol. XI,* 189.

130. John Wesley, *Works, Vol. XIII,* 133. The letter is dated May 2, 1786, and is addressed to "Mr. C."

131. John Wesley, *Works, Vol. X,* 83.

132. Cragg, 260. In *A Farther Appeal to Men of Reason and Religion, Part II.*

133. John Wesley, *Works, Vol. X,* 81. Excerpted from *A Letter to a Roman Catholic.*

134. Ward and Heitzenrater, *Journal and Diaries, Vol. 20,* 59-60.

135. Ibid., 296-297. From a letter received from Ireland on August 29, 1749.

136. Ibid., 331. Wesley's account of this is a result of meeting the woman at "Mr. P's" on April 12, 1750.

137. Ibid., 334. This occurred on April 30, 1750.

138. Cragg, 423. In *A Second Letter to the Author of the Enthusiasm of Methodists and Papists Compared,*" the first edition of which appeared in 1751. These recent conversions were fresh in Wesley's memory. See Cragg's stema of this letter's editions in Cragg, 556.

139. Wesley's relationship with Calvinists is addressed in: Albert Outler, *John Wesley,* 425-491; Alan Coppedge, *John Wesley in Theological Debate,* and W. Stephen Gunter, *The Limits of 'Love Divine': John Wesley's Response to Antinomianism and Enthusiasm*

(Nashville: Kingswood Books, 1989). Dallimore's biography of Whitefield covers his relationship with Calvinists, with Harry Stout's *Divine Dramatist* addressing it, but in less detail.

140. Whitefield, *Letters*, 98.

141. Ibid., 101.

142. Whitefield, *Journals*, 344.

143. Not only did the Tennant family make its own contribution in the persons of Gilbert, Charles, William, and William, Jr., but through the training facility at Neshaminy, Pennsylvania; the Log College, later Princeton, also contributed numerous other voices for the First Great Awakening. Notable among these is Samuel Davies, who carried the message of revival to the Southern Colonies. See Mark Noll, *A History of Christianity in the United States and Canada* (Grand Rapids: Eerdmans, 1992), 106, 111-112.

144. Whitefield, *Journals*, 476.

145. Ibid., 567.

146 Stout, 68-69. Also in Whitefield, *Letters*, 491-492, Letter VII.

147. Whitefield, *Letters*, 47. Letter XLIII, dated January 27, 1739.

148. Whitefield, *Journals*, 229.

149. Whitefield, *Letters*, 87. The letter was mailed from Philadephia after Whitefield disembarked. Many are dated November 10, 1739.

150. Ibid., 150. Letter CLXII.

151. Ibid., 210. Letter CCXX.

152. Ibid., 260. Letter CCLXXVI, dated April 28, 1741.

153. Ibid., 313. Letter CCCXLVI.

154. Ibid., 398. Letter CCCCXXI, dated May 29, 1742.

155. Ibid., 426. Letter CCCCXLVII.

156. Stout, 136.

157. Ibid., 136. Stout indicates that Whitefield was initially attracted to the "more radical dissenters." Finally, Whitefield threw his support behind the more moderate Calvinists.

158. Whitefield, *Letters*, 128-129. Letter CXXXVIII.

159. Ibid.,140. Letter CL, dated January 16, 1740. Written while Whitefield was in Savannah, Georgia.

160. Ibid., 262. Letter CCLXXX, dated May 16, 1741.

161. Ibid., 268. Letter CCLXXXVIII.

162. Ibid., 402. Letter CCCCXXV.

163. Stout argues convincingly, "Neither Whitefield's ecumenical theology nor his actor's instinct for center stage would allow him to be preempted by local concerns and interests, whether Presbyterian, Methodist, Baptist, or New World Separatist." Stout, 139.

164. John Wesley, *Works, Vol. X*, 351. Wesley's description of Calvin is found in *Some Remarks on "A Defense of the Preface to the Edinburgh Edition of Aspasio Vindicated."* The Servetus incident referred to by Wesley was an unfortunate one in the history of the Reformation in Geneva. Servetus had been condemned as a heretic by the Catholic Church for speaking out against the union of Church and state from the time of Constantine and for unorthodox views on the Nicene definition of the Trinity. He escaped the Inquisition, only to pass through Geneva, where he was arrested and charged with heresy. Calvin prepared the charges against him, even though some believed a Catholic heretic should be welcomed by Protestants. Servetus was convicted of heresy. Calvin recommended a humane execution, but Servetus was burned at the stake. See Justo L. Gonzalez. *The Story of*

Christianity, Vol. 2: The Reformation to the Present Day (San Francisco: Harper and Row, 1985), 67.

165. Cragg, 297. From *A Farther Appeal to Men of Reason and Religion, Part III.*

166. John Wesley, *Works, Vol. X*, 359.

167. Ibid., 361. From *The Question, "What is an Arminian?" Answered.*

168. Ward and Heitzenrater, *Journal and Diaries, Vol. 19*, 153. Journal entries are from June 19 and 20, 1740.

169. Cragg, 250-251.

170. Ibid., 252. From *A Farther Appeal to Men of Reason and Religion, Part II.*

171. John Wesley. *Works, Vol. VIII*, 300. From *Minutes of Several Conversations.*

172. Ibid., 328.

173. Ibid., 336-337.

174. Ibid., 285.

175. Ward and Heitzenrater, *Journal and Diaries, Vol. 19*, 72.

176. Ibid., 268. Wesley wrote that Harris issued a "pressing instance" for him to come to Wales to preach. Harris' letter reveals that Wesley did not stretch the truth! Harris wrote, "I believe it will be to the glory of God if you come to us, and if you could afford a considerable time, to go over South Wales. We are weak, and I am in hopes the Lord will send you with the fullness of the blessings of the gospel of peace, to cut us deeper, and to strengthen and root us in faith and love." Baker, *Letters, Vol. 26*, 5.

177. Ward and Heitzenrater, 341.

178. Baker, *Letters, Vol. 26*, 86.

179. Coppedge, 108.

180. Ward and Heitzenrater, *Journal and Diaries, Vol .22*, 99.

181. Ibid., 346.

182. Whitefield, *Letters*, 164-165. Of American Lutherans, Whitefield wrote, "Some of the Germans in America are holy souls, and deserve the character they bear. They keep up a close walk with God, and are remarkable for their sweetness and simplicity of behavior. They talk little, and think much. Most of them, I believe, are Lutherans. But where there is the image of my dear Master, there are my affections drawn." The key, of course, may have been their "talking little": There was no ground for controversy when the Lutherans (and others) kept their mouths shut. One Deist in particular, Benjamin Franklin, gained Whitefield's friendship, arguably one of the strongest friendships Whitefield ever had. But the fact that Franklin was instrumental in the dissemination of Whitefield's writings may have had a major role to play in that close relationship. More on this in Chapter 4.

183. The absence of the mention of the additional "great traditions" of Lutheranism and Eastern Orthodoxy may appear strange. Wesley had little to say about relations with Lutherans, and Whitefield's comments are limited to his contacts with them in America. Indeed, both Whitefield and Wesley were influenced by the stream of Lutheran Pietism, so indirectly, their relationship with Moravians can be examined as fellowship with "warm hearted" Lutherans. The following have examined Wesley's dependence on Orthodox theologians, but no evidence suggests he had personal contacts with those who followed Orthodoxy: Ted A. Campbell, *John Wesley and Christian Antiquity: Religious Vision and Cultural Changes* (Nashville: Kingswood Books, 1991); Luke L. Keefer, Jr., "John Wesley: Disciple of Early Christianity." Ph.D. dissertation, Temple University, 1982. That he valued "warm hearted" spirituality wherever he found it, few would argue.

184. Gabriel Fackre, *Ecumenical Faith in Evangelical Perspective* (Grand Rapids: Eerdmans, 1993), 16-17

Chapter 4

The Quest for Common Ground
within Methodism

George Whitefield and John Wesley both professed to having a catholic spirit. Their wide range of personal and professional friendships with those of varying traditions indicates that they endeavored to nurture such a spirit. Randy Maddox has argued that in Wesley's case, his catholic spirit serves as an example for those who seek to deepen "ecumenical cooperation" but are concerned about "sacrificing theological integrity."[1] The same could be said of Whitefield. Wesley believed that there were doctrines that were necessary for the salvation of one's soul, but that there were other doctrines, perhaps equally essential, that need not be discussed in theological dialogue, as they were agreed upon by all Christians of all persuasions.[2] Thus, John Wesley could write to a Roman Catholic and encourage fruitful dialogue even if the Council of Trent stood in the way of full fellowship. Likewise, George Whitefield, while less optimistic about Roman Catholic participation in the revival, did include Lutherans, Scottish Presbyterians, Anglicans, Quakers, Moravians, and others of vastly different opinions. If the "catholic spirits" of Whitefield and Wesley extended to such a wide range within the broader theological spectrum, why were they severely strained in including each other?

George Whitefield never scaled the heights of speculative theology. While Wesley would write treatises on original sin, predestination, and Christian perfection, Whitefield's ventures into theology were limited to his sermons. Wesley's role was often, if not largely, pastoral; Whitefield's always was. This is not to suggest that "right belief" was unimportant to Whitefield. He believed himself to be a fully orthodox son of the Church of England. Whitefield was convinced that God, in his sovereignty, had chosen certain individuals for salvation, who would be awakened to their need through the preaching of the gospel, and would be gifted with the faith necessary to respond to God's call to forgiveness. Theology was important to Whitefield inasmuch as it fit into this framework, and resulted in the pragmatic awakening of the elect to their promised reward.[3] In fact, Whitefield dreaded the proposition of Wesley coming to America, as God was empowering the preaching of Calvinistic preachers to catalyze the Great Awakening: "I dread your coming over to America; because the work of God is carried on here (and that in a most glorious manner) by doctrines quite opposite to those you hold."[4] The preaching of the doctrines of grace was "working." The proof of their effectiveness was obvious to Whitefield.

Yet pragmatism was not the only test for a "necessary" doctrine, as far as Whitefield was concerned. Wesley could produce witnesses to the effectiveness of the preaching of the universal availability of salvation and Christian perfection. These were doctrines against which Whitefield would rail. Of primary importance to Whitefield was the biblical basis of all essential doctrine. Whitefield argued that his beloved Calvinism was not a product of his reading Calvin, but of his reading of Scripture.[5] Further, Whitefield appealed to the Articles of the Church of England in support of his beliefs. His response to Wesley's sermon "Free Grace" reveals that he believed his Calvinism to fit naturally into the Anglican theological framework.[6] The argument can be made that Wesley considered the same three principles of Scriptural basis, accordance with the doctrine of the Church of England, and pragmatism as the necessary characteristic of the theological essential. Wesley was "willing to collaborate" within "a context that included a commitment to the ultimate authority of Scripture and to the theological formulations of the Church's understanding of the Bible contained in the Articles of Religion."[7] Both read the same Bible, both were ordained by the same Church, and both bore witness to the effectiveness of the gospel they preached. Their close relationship was strained by factors that would stretch the limits of evangelical ecumenicity, but would also strengthen the Methodist movement through its struggle to provide a theological consensus for all who sought holiness of both heart and life.

The Power of Publicity

Of the two principals of this study, George Whitefield was the more popular figure. His popularity as a preacher and leader of the revival spanned two continents. In North America, until the military and political heroics of George Washington, George Whitefield was the most popular "George" in the colonies. But his popularity was not solely based on his preaching abilities, for, regardless of the range of his itinerancy and the multitudes he addressed in both Europe and North America, a sizable portion of the population would never have heard the sound of his voice. Whitefield's genius included his ability to hold a crowd's attention and to coordinate the publicizing of the revival in the press on two continents.

Whitefield began his self-promotion when a young man of twenty-six years of age. While not a lifelong journal writer like Wesley, Whitefield's account of his early life, ministry, and numerous trips to North America found early and widespread distribution. The first authorized version of his *First Journal*, covering his first trip to America, was published by James Hutton, and went through several editions in 1738 alone. Whitefield followed the *First Journal* with an account of his childhood and professional training up to his ordination in 1735. He detailed the period between his ordination and the first trip to North America in *A Further Account of God's Dealings with the Reverend Mr. George Whitefield,* published in 1747. Whitefield revised them into one volume in

1756.[8] A portion of Whitefield's *Journals*, unpublished during his lifetime, was first published in 1938, but it only adds details of Whitefield's life until 1745.[9] The publication of the journals of one so young was grounds for accusation, and Whitefield regretted that "they were not deferred till after my death, or written by some other persons."[10] Yet by his own admission, after hearing from appreciative followers, he consented to their continued dissemination, "that those pious persons who have interceded in my behalf, may see what God, in answer to their prayers, has done for my soul" and that "the scoffers of these last days (may) mock on."[11]

Whitefield's published journals were only one piece of the publication puzzle. His letters to correspondents on two continents spread news of the revivals and the benevolent ministry of the orphanage in Savannah. They acted jointly as revival historiography and fund-raising appeal. He wrote from Boston in the fall of 1740, "Wonderful things are doing here. The word runs like lightning. Dagon daily falls before the ark."[12] In November he sent word to London:

At New York the Holy Ghost came down like a mighty rushing wind. At Baskenridge still a greater awakening among young and old. One that received Christ cried out, "He is come! He is come!" &c. The poor creature was wrapped up in the Lord Jesus: and both there and at New York my soul was taken almost out of the body. At Newark the Lord worked wonderfully amongst some young men; and here at Philadelphia the word runs very swiftly . . . . O that it was so at London![13]

Whitefield did not restrict his correspondence to supporters back in England. He had an extensive network of correspondents in North America as well.[14] As the representative letters show, they served as the means for encouraging revivals in other locales, and perhaps bred a bit of revival envy: "O that it was so in London!" However, these were not the only reasons for writing letters. They allowed Whitefield to keep the ministry of his beloved Bethesda Orphan House before the eyes of potential donors. From Savannah on February 29, 1740, he wrote, "The Orphan-house is in great forwardness. I feed near an hundred mouths daily, and am assured I serve a God who will supply all our wants. It would rejoice me to see you at Savannah, if your business will permit. I can now provide things convenient for your reception."[15]

In another letter that year he penned, "But our Lord still shows me, that the orphan-house will go on and flourish. It is often a great weight upon my soul; but through your and my dear friends prayers, the Lord I am persuaded will still support it."[16] Letters outlining the results of the revivals and those advertising the needs of the orphan house served the same purpose: word was spreading about what God was doing, and how he was using George Whitefield to accomplish it. "While the centerpiece of Whitefield's theology was the necessity of the new birth, the focus of his publicity campaign was on the success of his ministry."[17]

Whitefield's network of correspondents was useful in other ways. They "disseminated revival news by reprinting reports in local newspapers, relating progress to ministers, and distributing Whitefield's latest writings."[18] Preachers and newspapers provided Whitefield with some of his best advance publicity, and he "hogged the limelight and most of the column-inches."[19] Whitefield's strategy has been described as a "preach and print" approach, as the printed word was used to prepare prospective audiences to hear the preached word.[20] Still, the published reports in the contemporary press did more than merely advertise Whitefield as a coming attraction. They also provided his opponents with new ammunition for further debate. While the positive publicity was intentional, the opposition aroused by the negative helped fuel the revivals as well.

The colonial press allowed Whitefield to influence people in more than one place at a time. Not only could people follow the progress of the revival in other colonies, but they could consider purchasing Whitefield's printed works by reading advertisements, read one of his sermons, or follow the pamphlet debates waging between his supporters and detractors.[21] Whitefield's popularity naturally bred antagonism, especially among clergy of his own Anglican Church. Stout argues that Whitefield understood that "confrontation aroused curiosity," and both he and his traveling companion, William Seward, knew how to manipulate the press for their own benefit.[22]

Several instances support Stout's argument. In April 1740, Seward rented a Philadelphia ballroom that was a frequent haunt of Philadelphia society. The hall remained closed for only a short time until some who missed their times of merriment forced its reopening. Seward's propaganda told a different story. He suggested that Whitefield's preaching had made such an impact that even though the hall had been reopened, no one came to the festivities. This precipitated an argument in the press between Seward and William Bolton, the owner of the hall. Bolton suggested that the real reason behind the closure of the hall and the propaganda was that Seward and Whitefield constructed the incident as a publicity stunt. Word had already gone forth from Philadelphia to New York and Boston regarding the great change among Philadelphia's upper class, and Bolton believed it would not be long before news made it across the Atlantic. Seward apologized to Bolton, but the timing of the event was impeccable. By the time Whitefield arrived in Boston, opposition ministers refrained from speaking out against the Grand Itinerant, due in large part to the popularity he had cultivated through the use of the press.[23] The Boston press, however, benefitted from the ensuing controversy. Thomas Fleet, owner of the *Boston Evening Post* and opponent of the revival practices of Whitefield, indicated his pleasure in promoting such a debate that helped him sell newspapers.[24] From the summer of 1740 to the summer of 1741, over 30% of the editions of the *South Carolina Gazette* carried cover stories highlighting the debate between Whitefield's supporters and detractors.[25] The revival and the controversy it generated sold newspapers, so the publishers, many without intention, helped to fuel the revival.

America's foremost printer was part of the propaganda machine. Benjamin Franklin had been employed to print Whitefield's sermons and journals, and he proved to be a lifelong friend, although despite Whitefield's best efforts, he remained a Deist. Franklin noted that Whitefield used to pray for his conversion, "but never had the satisfaction of believing that his prayers were heard." Of their business relationship, Franklin notes:

> His writing and printing from time to time gave great advantage to his enemies; unguarded expressions, and even erroneous opinions, delivered in preaching might have been afterwards explained or qualifi'd by supposing others that might have accompani'd them, or they might have been denied, but *litera scripta manet.*[26]

Franklin did nothing to dissuade his friend from further publication, in fact, Franklin continued printing Whitefield's works. Immediately after critiquing Whitefield's rashness in sending materials to the printers, Franklin noted, "My business was now continually augmenting, and my circumstances growing daily easier, my newspaper having become very profitable, as being for a time almost the only one in this and the neighboring provinces."[27] On a personal level, Franklin may have wished his friend had more carefully edited his material destined for publication, but the pragmatic Franklin was glad for the revenue those works generated.

Whitefield was well aware of both the potential and the pitfalls that accompany popular acclaim. His passion for the stage never abated, and he understood that fine actors were well rewarded with a popular following. He recalled his early education at St. Mary de Crypt in Gloucester and how his eloquence and memory won him the honor of speaking before the corporation during their annual evaluation. During that stage of his life, Whitefield's love for acting grew, and he noted that he would often miss class for several days to better prepare himself for his roles. His schoolmaster wrote plays for him and his classmates, and with some chagrin, Whitefield notes he was often cast in female roles.[28] The stage exerted a tremendous influence on Whitefield, and whether he fully comprehended it or not, "drama informed his sense of destiny."[29]

Whitefield was also aware of the dangers of such popularity. On his first trip to North America he wrote to Rev. Ebenezer Pemberton, apologizing for not acting with the proper humility due an elder.[30] He explains this by adding, ". . . you know, reverend Sir, how difficult it is to meet with success, and not be puffed up with it, and therefore if any such thing was discernible in my conduct, oh pity me, and pray to the Lord to heal my pride. All I can say is, that I desire to learn of Jesus Christ to be meek and lowly in heart; but my corruptions are so strong, and my employ so dangerous, that sometimes I am afraid."[31] In another letter to Pemberton later in 1739, Whitefield thanked several individuals "for what they did on my account," and notes, "Alas, I fear they think too highly of me. Oh dear Sir, entreat the God of all grace to give me humility, so shall success not prove my ruin."[32] From the perspective of some, this prayer was not answered quickly enough. After Whitefield wrote his stinging response to John Wesley's sermon "Free Grace," Susanna Wesley took pen in hand and wrote, *Some Remarks on a Letter from the Rev. Mr. Whitefield to the Rev. Mr. Wesley, In a Letter from a Gentlewoman to her Friend*. Defending her son, she wrote of Whitefield:

> He appeared young in the world and was not apprized that popular applause had such an intoxicating quality, that few men have heads strong enough to bear it. Nor did he consider that praise is the most contagious breath, nor knew that the sails of native pride are ever ready to receive such winds, which frequently increase a man's sins, but never add one cubit to the stature of his worth.[33]

She further accused Whitefield of having an ego bruised by the popularity her sons Charles and John had attained by the time Whitefield returned to England from his first North American visit:

> . . . he found the Wesleys were men of an established reputation among the better sort of people for the purity of their doctrine and integrity of their lives . . . and as he too much affected popularity himself, as appears in some of his writings, he might probably think his own glory suffered some diminution by the increase of their reputation.[34]

These observations could be dismissed as the writings of a loving mother attempting to defend her wounded children. Nevertheless, Whitefield's letters to Pemberton suggest that the lure of the spotlight and the roar of popular applause were a constant temptation in his own mind. For even by the time he arrived in North America the first time, "Whitefield had carefully crafted a view of himself as a special instrument elected by God to proclaim the necessity of the new birth. Writing in promotional language as well as in theological discourse, Whitefield presented himself as a well-publicized success 'recently arrived from England.'"[35] He would continue to make his personal successes as an evangelist a key marketing strategy.[36]

Whitefield had known success as a revivalist in England, but had left and found even greater popularity in North America. Upon his return to England, he found the Wesleys occupying the place of leadership in the revivals he once held. Bruised ego aside, Whitefield employed a proven strategy: open dissemination of his views in a confrontational style that would reintroduce his name to his public. Wesley chose to "preach and print" his sermon "Free Grace," which set him up as the champion of the unlimited atonement of Christ. Whitefield published his reply to Wesley's sermon, not only to reestablish his popularity, but also to highlight what he felt were glaring theological problems with Wesley's sermon. In doing so, Whitefield became the champion of the Calvinistic evangelicals. Lines were drawn in the sand that both Wesley and Whitefield would later erase, but which their followers would dig ever deeper.

The Theological Issue

The publication of Whitefield's response to Wesley's sermon brought to public attention a theological issue that had been simmering in private correspondence for some time. On July 2, 1739, Whitefield wrote to Wesley, having found himself in a dilemma. He felt pulled between his friendship with Wesley and his commitment to Calvinistic theology. He questioned Wesley, "How shall I tell the Dissenters I do not approve of their doctrines, without wronging my own soul? How shall I tell them I do, without contradicting my honoured friend, whom I desire to love as my own soul? Lord, for Thy infinite mercy's sake, direct me so to act, as neither to injure myself nor my friend!"[37] The next month, after seeking divine guidance by casting a lot, Wesley printed his sermon "Free Grace." Before word reached Whitefield, who had left on his second trip to North America, he wrote to his friend in England regarding the differences that were coming to light. Citing Christian perfection, election, and the perseverance of the saints as the key doctrines on which they differed, he encouraged Wesley to drop the issue and to remain silent about the differences. Whitefield explained that he was "ten thousand times more convinced" of his belief in election and the perseverance of the saints than when he last saw Wesley. "You think otherwise," Whitefield argues, "why then should we dispute, when there is no probability of convincing? Will it not in the end destroy brotherly love, and insensibly take from us that cordial union and sweetness of soul, which I pray God may always subsist between us?"[38]

Whitefield had already determined the outcome of the public debate. While he could not control the responses of other Calvinists, he could control his own. He already concluded how he would respond. Whitefield wrote to James Hutton on June 7, 1740, "For Christ's sake desire dear Brother Wesley to avoid disputing with me. I think I had rather die, than to see a division between us; and yet, how can we walk together, if we oppose each other?"[39] Whitefield placed the blame for the crisis squarely on Wesley's shoulders, but wasn't he equally responsible? His letters suggest that he had no choice but to respond openly and decisively. Yet Whitefield had seen firsthand the value of controversy to the furtherance of the revivals in North America. Perhaps a tiff with Wesley would provide similar results in England.

Missing from Whitefield's correspondence with Wesley during the time of their division is an appreciation for the integrity of Wesley's theological position. It is as if Whitefield could not see the vast "forest" of God's grace for the "trees" representing his Calvinism. Whitefield believed he had every right to express his Calvinism, but how dare Wesley question the doctrines of grace? In his letter of March 26, 1740, Whitefield had encouraged Wesley not to dispute in public with him on the issues upon which they differed. But later, in the same correspondence, Whitefield wrote, "Honoured Sir, let us offer salvation freely to all by the blood of Jesus; and whatever light God has communicated to us, let us freely communicate to others."[40] At one time, he recommended that he and Wesley preach the gospel in all its simplicity but also allowed that each of them should enhance their preaching with additional light as God reveals it. Thus, along with the evangelistic preaching that was a common denominator of the leaders of Methodism, Whitefield had left open the door for the continuation of his Calvinistic preaching, while also making allowance for Wesley's preaching of the unlimited atonement.

In a follow-up letter dated May 24, Whitefield tried to convince Wesley of the truth of Calvinistic doctrine. "The writings of the most experienced men, and the experiences of the most established Christians," coupled with the pragmatic example of the Great Awakening that was being "carried on" in America "by doctrines quite opposite" those of Wesley, further convinced Whitefield of the truth of the doctrines of grace. God taught the American divines the doctrine of election; Wesley, Whitefield implied, should learn from the same source. "If I mistake not," Whitefield stated hopefully, "dear and honoured Mr. Wesley hereafter will be convinced also."[41] Whitefield changed his tone by June 25, the date of his next letter to Wesley. A few months prior he suggested that he and Wesley be allowed to preach "whatever light God has communicated to us." Now he emphatically proclaimed, "For Christ's sake, if possible, dear Sir, never speak against election in your sermons: no one can say that I ever mentioned it in public discourses, whatever my private sentiments may be."[42] That Whitefield held Calvinistic doctrines privately, few would dispute. His contention that he was not preaching those doctrines openly is debatable.

At the least, Whitefield was becoming more assured of the truth of Calvinism. He admitted this in his letters. Further evidence is found in the relationships he was cultivating in North America. He mentioned various Independents, Presbyterians, and Dissenters in general, and the Tennants in particular.[43] He preached to various Dissenting and Independent congregations who would have expected to hear Calvinistic doctrine preached from their pulpits. After preaching in a Baptist meeting house on March 15, Whitefield indicated that recently, a person preached from that pulpit "who denied the doctrine of original sin, the Divinity and Righteousness of our Lord, and the operation of God's Blessed Spirit upon the soul." In his sermon, Whitefield "was led to shew the utter inability of man to save himself, and absolute necessity of his dependence on the rich mercies and free grace of God in Christ Jesus for his restoration;" standards of Whitefield's Calvinism.[44] Within days, he noted how pleased he was that numerous seekers were "desirous . . . of laying hold on and having an interest in the complete and everlasting righteousness of the Lord Jesus Christ."[45] On May 8, he preached to a congregation, attempting to clear himself "from some aspersions that had been cast upon my doctrine, as though it tended to antinomianism."[46] Interestingly, one of Wesley's major criticisms of Whitefield's Calvinism was the fact that the doctrine of election could lead to practical antinomianism. If an individual is elected, "do what they will," where was the motivation for holiness of both heart and life? Since Whitefield was now being accused of antinomianism, it is logical to conclude that he was espousing Calvinistic doctrine in public.

In fact, by 1740, Whitefield was indeed preaching Calvinistic doctrine. His sermon "The Lord our Righteousness" was preached on September 11, 1741, in the High Church Yard of Glasgow. A publisher's note indicates that "the substance of the following sermon was delivered at the Old South Church in Boston, October, 1740."[47] The sermon was a basic argument for the imputed righteousness of Christ in the life of the believer. His introductory statement is telling: ". . . we would, if not wholly, yet in part at least, glory in being the cause of our own salvation . . . . We cry out against popery, and that very justly; but we are all Papists; at least, I am sure, we are all Arminians by nature; and, therefore, no wonder so many natural men embrace that scheme."[48] In confronting the argument often lodged against Calvinists, that teaching the imputed righteousness of Christ leads to antinomianism, Whitefield accused Arminians of being the most lawless, remarking that Arminian beliefs, being unchristian beliefs, led to sinful behavior.[49] He concluded by again grouping Arminians and Roman Catholics together:

I observed at the beginning of this discourse, that we were all Arminians and Papists by nature; for, as one says, "Arminianism is the back way to popery." And here I venture further to affirm, that if we deny the doctrine of an imputed righteousness, whatever we may style ourselves, we are really Papists in our hearts, and deserve no other title from men.[50]

Additional evidence that Whitefield was overtly preaching Calvinistic doctrine while he informed Wesley to the contrary is provided from the press of Benjamin Franklin. In 1740, Franklin published a two-volume set of Whitefield's sermons.[51] The two volumes contain twenty-two of Whitefield's sermons that, if they had not been publicly preached, were at least made available to the reading public. Hence, any Calvinistic doctrine contained in any of those printed sermons could not be defended as having been "kept quiet." Included in this publication was Whitefield's sermon "What Think ye of Christ?" Here, Whitefield employed his standard attack on Arminianism, namely that it assumed God foresaw certain "work or fitness" in an individual, hence making the individual in part responsible for his or her salvation.[52] Whitefield continued the sermon by clearly expressing Calvinistic doctrine, particularly election, which in the June 25, 1740 letter, he admitted to holding only privately:

> Our salvation is all of God, from the beginning to the end; it is not of works, lest any man should boast; man has no hand in it: it is Christ who is to be made to us of God the Father, wisdom, righteousness, sanctification, and eternal redemption . . . . Not that you must think God will save you because, or on account of your faith; for (then) faith is a work, and then you would be justified for your works; but when I tell you, we are to be justified by faith, I mean that faith is the instrument whereby the sinner applies or brings home the redemption of Jesus Christ to his heart. *And to whomsoever God gives such a faith, (for it is the free gift of God)* he may lift up his head with boldness, he need not fear . . . it is not a faith of the head only, but a faith of the heart. It is a living principle *wrought in the soul, by the Spirit of the ever-living God*, convincing the sinner of his lost, undone condition by nature; *enabling him to apply and lay hold on the perfect righteousness of Jesus Christ*, freely offered him in the gospel . . .[53]

He spoke later of the "effectual call" of Saul, and of how his hearers should "beg of God to make you willing to be saved in this day of power; for it is not flesh and blood, but the Spirit of Jesus Christ, that alone can reveal these things unto you." And in his closing invitation, he addressed those wondering if they had been called, "If you say, you cannot believe, you say right; for faith, as well as every other blessing, is the gift of God; but then wait upon God, and who knows but he may have mercy upon thee?"[54]

Also included in Whitefield's collection published by Franklin was the sermon "Of Justification by Christ." Here Whitefield explained the concept of justification, taught that "all mankind in general, and every individual person in particular" stood in need of being justified, and that the only way for one to be justified was through the finished work of Christ. In doing so, he highlighted his belief in election and the limited atonement of Christ:

> "As by the disobedience of one man, judgment came upon all men unto condemnation;" or all men were condemned on having Adam's sin imputed to them; "so by the obedience of one, that is, Jesus Christ, the free gift of pardon and peace came upon all men, (all sorts of men) unto justification of life." I say all sorts of men; for the apostle in this chapter is only drawing a parallel between the first and second Adam in this respect, that they acted both as representatives; and as the posterity of Adam had his sin imputed to them, so those for whom Christ died, and whose representative he is, shall have his merits imputed to them also. Whoever runs the parallel farther, in order to prove universal redemption (whatever arguments they may draw for the proof of it from other passages of scripture,) if they would draw one from this for that purpose, I think they stretch their line of interpretation beyond the limits of scripture.[55]

Whitefield's claim that he "never mentioned (election) in public discourses" would have been technically accurate if these sermons were never preached in public. But his views on the subject were being disseminated publicly, much as Wesley's views on the unlimited atonement were as well. Incidentally, Whitefield encouraged those who shared his views on election not to make it an issue for public debate. Writing to a leading woman in a society in Bristol, Whitefield instructed, "The doctrines of election, and of final perseverance, I hold as well as you. But then, they are not to be contended for with heat and passion. Such a proceeding will only prejudice the cause you would defend. Pray shew this to your other friends."[56]

In Whitefield's defense, the doctrine of election, while vitally important to him, took up only a small portion of his preaching time. Yet it seemed to be a key factor in the division between him and Wesley. At times in his writings, Whitefield painted basic Calvinism in such glowing colors as to make acceptance of Calvinism necessary for saving faith. In a letter dated November 10, 1739, he wrote:

Oh the excellency of the doctrine of election, and of the saints final perseverance, to those who are truly sealed by the spirit of promise! I am persuaded, till a man comes to believe and feel these important truths, he cannot come out of himself; but when convinced of these, and assured of the application of them to his own heart, he then walks by faith indeed, not in himself, but in the Son of God, who died and gave himself for him.[57]

These instances are, however, rare. More typical of Whitefield was an appeal to basic beliefs common to both Calvinistic evangelicals and Wesleyan Arminians as necessary elements of true Christianity. In comparing the wise and foolish virgins of Matthew 25, he noted that the difference between them was that the foolish virgins with empty oil lamps signified individuals with "no principle of a true living faith and holiness in their hearts."[58] Elsewhere he spoke of the importance of knowing the power of Christ's resurrection "experimentally," of having received the Holy Ghost, and by the power of the Holy Ghost, being "raised from the death of sin, to a life of righteousness, and true holiness."[59] Most basic to Whitefield's belief system was the "necessity of being justified in (God's) sight by faith only."[60] By early 1738, the doctrine of the New Birth had become for Whitefield "a subject on which" he delighted "to dwell."[61] Later that spring, on his first trip to North America, Whitefield rejoiced in the conversations that went on in the great cabin, ". . . scarce a word is to be heard amongst us when together, but what has reference to our fall in the first, and our new birth in the Second Adam, the Lord from Heaven."[62] He later wrote, "Pure and undefiled religion consists in a lively faith in Jesus Christ, as the only mediator between God and man. A faith that changes and renews the whole soul, takes it entirely off the world, and fixes it wholly upon God."[63] John Wesley himself recognized the overarching emphases in Whitefield's ministry, when, in giving one of the many sermons preached after Whitefield's death he proclaimed, "You are not ignorant that these are the fundamental doctrines which he everywhere insisted on. And may they not be summed up, as it were, in two words — the new birth, and justification by faith?"[64]

John Wesley was no less convinced of the necessity of the New Birth and justification by faith. In his tribute to Whitefield he proclaimed:

These let us insist upon with all boldness, at all times, and in all places; in public (those of us who are called thereto) and, at all opportunities, in private. Keep close to these good, old, unfashionable doctrines, how many soever contradict and blaspheme. Go on, my brethren, "in the name of the Lord, and in the power of his might," with all care and diligence "keep that safe which is committed to your trust;" knowing that "heaven and earth shall pass away; but" this truth "shall not pass away."[65]

For Wesley, the basics of the Christian faith could be reduced to a few essentials. In his *The Character of a Methodist*, Wesley succinctly defined salvation as "holiness of heart and life."[66] Further, a genuine Methodist "is one who has 'the love of God shed abroad in his heart by the Holy Ghost given unto him;' one who 'loves the Lord his God with all his heart, and with all his soul, and with all his mind, and with all his strength.'"[67] True Methodists possess spiritual contentment, willingly give thanks, live a life of prayer, do the will of the Father, keep his commandments, do all to the glory of God, and do good unto all. Regardless of one's denomination, if they are in agreement with these principles, Wesley considered them "Methodists." Wesley assumed his reader would draw the obvious conclusion: that the Methodists were merely practitioners of "the common fundamental principles of Christianity."[68] Wesley further described "plain, old Christianity" as being evidenced in the life of one who:

> . . . is inwardly and outwardly conformed to the will of God, as revealed in the written word. He thinks, speaks, and lives, according to the method laid down in the revelation of Jesus Christ. His soul is renewed after the image of God, in righteousness and in all true holiness. And having the mind that was in Christ, he so walks as Christ also walked.[69]

Not only were these the distinguishing marks of a Methodist, but the distinguishing characteristics of all Christian believers of any denomination. Scholars have begun to interpret Wesley as holding "essential" doctrines on two different levels. The first level has been described as the cognitive level. Thomas describes these as "those fundamental, rational truths which distinguished Christianity as a body of truth from that which was not Christianity."[70] Maddox affirms that the defining doctrines of Christianity, those that were assented to by all Christians everywhere, were considered to be essential.[71] The doctrine of the Trinity was just such a doctrine, as it was one of the distinctive Christian beliefs. It was a "cognitive theological truth" that was "absolutely integral to the identity of Christianity as Christianity."[72] These were the doctrines of Wesley's beloved Church of England, and of every fellowship dedicated to standard Christian doctrine.

Wesley also subscribed to doctrines that he considered essential on another level. These were doctrines that Wesley believed to be essential to one's experiential salvation. Maddox suggests that there were four key doctrines that Wesley emphasized far more than others: original sin, justification by faith, the New Birth, and holiness of heart and life.[73] On the experiential level, a theological essential was that which "had a direct and necessary relation to personal salvation."[74] Thomas argues that these doctrines were both clearly revealed in Scripture and had to be "experienced" by one's spiritual senses.[75] "In Wesley's mind an essential doctrine was one vital to salvation. Everything else represented speculative theory, and therefore held a very marginal place in his interest."[76] Thus, Wesley could write in his *A Plain Account of the People Called Methodists*, ". . . orthodoxy, or right opinions, is, at best, but a very slender part of religion, if it can be allowed to be any part of it at all."[77] Elsewhere Wesley wrote, "The distinguishing marks of a Methodist are not his opinions of any sort . . . . as to all opinions which do not strike at the root of Christianity, we think and let think."[78] A common cognitive theology bound all Christians together; a common experiential theology provided grounds for agreement between Methodists and like-minded evangelicals. For a few years, even such elementary basics could not keep Whitefield and Wesley united.

Catholic Spirit: Strained and Regained

George Whitefield and John Wesley both claimed to possess a catholic spirit. Wesley even pointed this out as one of Whitefield's defining characteristics.[79] But Whitefield, who carried out cordial relationships with certain Anglicans, Dissenters, and Deists, and Wesley, whose relationships were no less diverse, struggled through several years of a severely strained friendship. This occurred even though they were agreed on the fundamental doctrines of justification by faith and the New Birth. From 1739 until 1741, two Methodists who preached the same simple gospel found a catholic spirit nearly impossible to cultivate between themselves.

Throughout his ministry, Whitefield was outspoken regarding his possession of a catholic spirit. From Margate on January 9, 1738, he wrote, "I would willingly be of so catholic a spirit, as to love the image of my divine master, wherever I see it: I am far from thinking God's grace is confined to any set of men whatsoever . . . and therefore his benefits are not to be confined to this or that particular set of professors."[80] On August 3, 1739, he penned, "I love all that love our Lord Jesus Christ. The spirit of Christ, with me is the center. I love the man, and you in particular, though in all things he may not follow with me."[81] In one of the many letters posted from Philadelphia on November 10, 1739, Whitefield praised an individual who disagreed with him on certain issues, but was in agreement with him on essential doctrine:

> I wish all names among the saints of God were swallowed up in that one of Christian. I long for professors to leave off placing religion in saying "I am a Churchman," "I am a Dissenter." My language to such is, "Are you of Christ? If so, I love you with all my heart:" for this reason chiefly, dear Sir, my heart is drawn out toward you.[82]

Accompanying this letter was one that continued the theme. "My one sole question is, Are you a Christian? Are you sealed by Christ's spirit to the day of redemption? Are you hungering and thirsting after the perfect, everlasting righteousness of Jesus Christ? If so, you are my brother, my sister and mother."[83] Whitefield was attracted to a catholic spirit wherever he found it. He wrote to Benjamin Coleman, praising him for exhibiting such a spirit. He continued, "O that bigotry and party zeal were not so much as once named amongst us, as becometh saints! Since Christ is not divided in himself, why should Christians be divided one amongst another? Bigotry, I am sure, can never be the fruit of that wisdom which cometh from above."[84]

The friendship between George Whitefield and John Wesley went further than simply being the fruit of their catholic spirits. Friends since their days at Oxford, Whitefield's early correspondence to Wesley is marked by deep respect and references to Wesley as his "spiritual father in Christ."[85] He continued the deferential language in letters written to Wesley through early 1739. On March 23, Whitefield wrote expectantly that while Wesley would follow him at Bristol, that he would be preferred before him. Two weeks later Whitefield encouraged Wesley by wishing him "all the success imaginable" in his ministry at Bristol.[86]

The first sign of strain in their relationship appeared in a letter Whitefield wrote dated June 25, 1739. Writing from London, Whitefield appealed to Wesley:

> I hear, honoured sir, that you are about to print a sermon against predestination. It shocks me to think of it. What will be the consequences but controversy? If people ask my opinion, what shall I do? I have a critical part to act. God enable me to behave aright! Silence on both sides will be best. It is noised abroad already that there is a division between you and me, and my heart within me is grieved.[87]

The gravity of Whitefield's dilemma is evident in the follow-up letter he sent to Wesley the following week. Arguing that the peace of the church was at stake, he pleaded with Wesley not to publish his sermon on free grace. Yet in the same paragraph he indicated his desire for the success of Wesley's ministry, hoping that Wesley might "increase" while he might "decrease."[88]

Both of these letters were written after the fact. Wesley had already preached the sermon publicly, and the publication of it was soon to follow. Whitefield's distress over the publication of *Free Grace* is apparent in the three letters he wrote to Wesley during the spring and summer of 1740.[89] On August 9, Wesley responded to the letter Whitefield had written on May 24. Wesley honestly assessed their differences, but the general tone of the letter was positive:

> The case is quite plain. There are bigots both for Predestination and against it. God is sending a message to those on either side. But neither will receive it, unless from one of his own opinion. Therefore for a time you are suffered to be of one opinion and I of another. But when His time is come God will do what man cannot - namely, make us both of one mind. Then persecution will flame out, and it will be seen whether we count our lives dear unto ourselves so that we may finish our course with joy.[90]

Before receiving this letter, Whitefield wrote to Wesley, "O that God may give you a sight of his free, sovereign, and electing love! But no more of this: why will you compel me to write thus? Why will you dispute? I am willing to go with you to prison, and to death; but I am not willing to oppose you."[91] Frank Baker senses "a heavy destiny" in Whitefield's letter of November 24.[92] He wrote:

> O that there may be harmony, and very intimate union between us! Yet it cannot be, since you hold universal Redemption. But no more of this . . . . The children of God are disunited among themselves. The king of the church shall yet over-rule all things for good. My dear brother, for Christ's sake avoid all disputation. Do not oblige me to preach against you; I had rather die.[93]

Whitefield's next letter was a lengthy polemic aimed at correcting the false doctrine Wesley was preaching. Dated December 24, it was the letter that was subsequently published in response to Wesley's public denunciation of election.[94] In a follow-up letter dated February 1, 1741, Whitefield informed Wesley that the December 24 letter was in publication at Charleston and Boston, and that he was bringing to England a copy to be published there. In one of the unique twists of history, on the very day that Whitefield wrote those words, Wesley was presiding at a meeting at the Foundery. An advance copy of Whitefield's lengthy letter had been covertly printed for distribution at the Foundery that day. Upon discovering the tract, Wesley announced to the gathering that he intended to do with it what Whitefield would do, and promptly tore up his copy, encouraging the congregation to do the same.[95]

Now the rift between Whitefield and Wesley was apparent on both sides of the Atlantic. From February through October of 1741, no written correspondence passed between them. Upon Whitefield's return to England, Wesley attended one of his meetings to hear for himself Whitefield's opinion of Wesley.

In his *Journal*, Wesley recorded, "I much approved of his plainness of speech. He told me, he and I preached two different gospels, and therefore he not only would not join with, or give me the right hand of fellowship, but was resolved publicly to preach against me and my brother, wheresoever he preached at all." Any promise he had made to keep his opinion concerning Wesley quiet, was "only an effect of human weakness," and that he had changed his mind.[96] Within a few days, Wesley recorded somberly that Whitefield "had said enough of what was wholly foreign to the question, to make an open (and probably irreparable) breach between him and me: Seeing 'for a treacherous wound, and for the be-wraying of secrets, every friend will depart.'"[97] Those words proved prophetic for the Methodist movement in general, but the Catholic spirits and friendship of the two key leaders of the movement proved more powerful than the forces that drew them apart.

Whitefield made the first move toward reconciliation. Writing to Wesley on October 10, 1741, he apologized for revealing the manner in which Wesley determined to publish his sermon *Free Grace*. After seeking Wesley's forgiveness, Whitefield continued, "I find I love you as much as ever, and pray God, if it be his blessed will, that we may be all united together . . . . May God remove all obstacles that now prevent our union! Though I hold particular election, yet I offer Jesus freely to every individual soul . . . . May all disputings cease . . ."[98] He wrote to T.E. on November 27 of his intention "not to rest till every thing, contrary to true, catholic, christian love, be rooted out of my soul. Christ's blood and spirit are able to do this for me. I only need to pray to God to make me willing to have it done."[99] To another correspondent, he wrote on January 2, 1742, "Brother Robert, it is a blessed thing to have always a Catholic spirit. I am persuaded, Jesus will give it to me. I am resolved never to rest, 'till self-love, bigotry, prejudice, and all narrowness of spirit be expelled out of my soul."[100] The following month in a letter to Thomas Noble, Whitefield penned:

> Before (your letter) came, the Lord had given me an enlarged heart, and unfeigned love and freedom to converse with all his dear children, of whatever denomination I talk freely with the Messrs. Wesley, though we widely differ in a certain point. Most talk of a catholic spirit; but it is only till they have brought people into the pale of their own church. This is downright sectarianism, not catholicism. How can I act consistently, unless I receive and love all the children of God, whom I esteem to be such, of whatever denomination they may be? Why should we dispute when there is no probability of convincing? I think this is not giving up the faith, but fulfilling our Lord's new command, "Love one another:" and our love is but feigned, unless it produces proper effects. I am persuaded, the more the love of God is shed abroad in our hearts,

the more all narrowness of spirit will subside and give way: besides, so far as we are narrow spirited, we are uneasy. Prejudices, jealousies, and suspicions make the soul miserable, so far as they are entertained.[101]

Wesley apprehended the irenic spirit Whitefield was exhibiting. After spending "an agreeable hour" with Whitefield, Wesley noted in his *Journal* that he believed Whitefield to be sincere "concerning his earnest desire of joining hand in hand with all that love the Lord Jesus Christ." He added rather cryptically, "But if (as some would persuade me) he is not, the loss is all on his own side. I am just as I was: I go on my way, whether he goes with me or stays behind."[102] By August 1743, Wesley, too, had a "strong desire to unite with Mr. Whitefield as far as possible," and endeavored to "cut off needless dispute" by condensing his thought on the "three points in debate: 1. Unconditional Election. 2. Irresistible Grace. 3. Final Perseverance." Written in his personal *Journal*, Wesley attempted to go as far as possible to meet Whitefield on common ground. As to election, Wesley admits, "And I do not deny, (though I cannot prove it is so,) that (God) had unconditionally elected some persons to eternal glory." Regarding irresistible grace, Wesley conceded, "The grace which brings faith, and thereby salvation into the soul, is irresistible at that moment." On the subject of final perseverance Wesley was "inclined" to believe, "That there is a state attainable in this life, from which a man cannot finally fall: And that he has attained this, who can say, 'Old things are passed away; all things' in me 'are become new.'"[103] Far from robbing his theological system of integrity, Wesley was endeavoring to provide grounds for a basic consensus upon which the Methodist revival, which both Whitefield and Wesley intended to be carried on based upon terms of evangelical ecumenicity, could continue.

The rebuilding of their relationship and the defense of each other's ministries continued until Whitefield's death. In *A Farther Appeal to Men of Reason and Religion, Part I*, first published in 1743, Wesley responded to the accusations that Wesley and Whitefield did not agree on doctrinal issues, nor could they carry on a cordial relationship. Responding to the first accusation, Wesley argued that on every "fundamental doctrine," he and Whitefield had agreed for several years. "In these we hold one and the same thing. In smaller points each of us thinks and lets think." Addressing the second accusation, Wesley encouraged the reader to examine what Whitefield wrote, "even in the heat of controversy, and he will be convinced of the contrary." He next denied any animosity on his part toward Whitefield, stating, "I reverence Mr. Whitefield, both as a child of God and a true minister of Jesus Christ," believing that both he and Whitefield were fully led by the Holy Spirit.[104] Between January 19 and 21, 1750, Whitefield and Wesley traded preaching and liturgical responsibilities at the chapel in West-Street, with Wesley commenting on the event, "So, by the blessing of God, one more stumbling-block is removed." The following week

Wesley gloried in the wisdom of God, in granting different gifts to him and Whitefield, that one could reach those that the other could not.[105]

Within five years their relationship had been healed to the point that Wesley could write on November 5, 1755, "Mr. Whitefield called upon me; disputings are now no more: We love one another, and join hand in hand to promote the cause of our common Master."[106] Still later, Wesley commended Whitefield for the role he was playing in healing the "first breach among the Methodists." "Mr. B. called upon me, now calm and in his right mind," wrote Wesley, "God has repressed his furious, bitter zeal, by means of Mr. Whitefield." And at the end of the same month he noted, "Mr. Whitefield called upon me. He breathes nothing but peace and love. Bigotry cannot stand before him, but hides its head wherever he comes."[107] The following year, he wrote to Mrs. Emma Moon, "In every place where Mr. Whitefield has been, he has labored in the same friendly, Christian manner. God has indeed effectually broken down the wall of partition which was between us. Thirty years ago we were one: Then the sower of tares rent us asunder: But now a stronger than him has made us one again."[108]

Whitefield also continued to encourage and embody a catholic spirit throughout the remainder of his life. On August 1, 1741, Whitefield wrote to Rev. Gabriel Wilson, "O that my heart glowed with the love of God and men! I would breathe nothing but love. I would love all that love the Lord Jesus, of whatsoever denomination. May the Lord heal our divisions, and grant that we may not thereby provoke him to send us a common persecution to drive us together."[109] The following year he corresponded with Mr. J.N., encouraging him to nurture a Catholic spirit within himself:

> I want to be more like unto Jesus, God blessed for evermore! who sees all the quarrels and heart-risings of his children one amongst another, and yet bears with, and loves them still. My heart doth not reproach me, for my kindness and friendship with those that differ from me. I think I have been led by the word and spirit of God into this part of my conduct . . . . My principles as to the fundamentals of the gospel are just the same as yours. I cannot renounce those precious truths, that I have felt the power of, and which were taught me not of man but of God. At the same time, I would love all that love Jesus, though they differ from me in some points. The angels love all the true worshippers of Jesus every where, and why should not we? If our brethren will quarrel with us, let us not quarrel with them.[110]

To Mr. F. in Philadelphia, Whitefield wrote a revealing letter:

But blessed be God, matters are brought to a better issue, and though we cannot agree in principles, yet we agree in love. Tho', as you know, I am clear in the truths of the gospel, yet I find that principles of themselves, without the spirit of God, will not unite any set of men whatever; and where the spirit of God is in any great degree, there will be union of heart, though there may be difference in sentiments. This I have learnt, my dear brother, by happy experience, and find great freedom and peace in my soul thereby. This makes me to love many, though I cannot agree with them in some of their principles. I dare not look upon them as wilful deceivers, but as persons who hazard their lives for the sake of the gospel. Mr. W. (Wesley?) I think is wrong in some things, and Mr. L. wrong also; yet I believe that both Mr. L. and Mr. W., and others, with whom we do not agree in all things, will shine bright in glory. It is best therefore for a gospel-minister, simply and powerfully to preach those truths he has been taught of God, and to meddle as little as possible with those who are children of God, though they should differ in many things.[111]

For Whitefield, he would "bear and converse with all others, who do not err in fundamentals, and who give evidence that they are true lovers of the Lord Jesus. This is what I mean by a catholic spirit."[112] Whitefield's catholic spirit was to be admired, "for always unity of Christian spirit and service — not conformity of creed and ritual — was his guiding principle . . ."[113]

Wesley, no less than Whitefield, encouraged and embodied a catholic spirit. Not only was a Catholic spirit something he valued in others, as witnessed by Whitefield's funeral sermon, but he sought to cultivate it in his own life and in the lives of his followers. First preached in 1750, Wesley's sermon "A Caution Against Bigotry" sought to caution hearers against the dangers of a party spirit.[114] Wesley's basic premise was that God's work of calling people to repentance and salvation would be carried out by members of various denominations, and that those who consider their denomination the "true Church" must be careful to acknowledge that God will work through faithful, warm-hearted believers of any denomination. There may be those who differ in "religious opinions" who are faithfully calling people into the Kingdom of God.

Wesley indicated that his hearers should not be surprised at the multiplication of "opinions" nor that differences between proponents of them had arisen:

There was a time when all Christians were of one mind, as well as of one heart. So great grace was upon them all when they were first filled with the Holy Ghost. But how short a space did this blessing continue! How soon was that unanimity lost, and difference of opinion sprang up again, even in the church of Christ! And that not in nominal but in real Christians; nay, in the very chief of them, the apostles themselves! Nor does it appear that the difference which then began was ever entirely removed.[115]

Wesley continued by admitting that it was quite probable that whenever one witnessed another doing the work of God, that individual would not be of the same opinion as the witness: "'Tis scarce to be imagined he will be of our mind in all points, even of religion. He may very probably think in a different manner from us even on several subjects of importance, such as the nature and use of the moral law, the eternal decrees of God, the sufficiency and efficacy of his grace, and the perseverance of his children."[116] It is interesting to note the "opinions" Wesley used to illustrate those beliefs on which Christians often disagree. In addressing a Christian's response to the moral law, God's decrees, the extent of the atonement, and final perseverance, Wesley addressed the basic areas of doctrinal disagreement between Arminians and Calvinists. Clearly, Wesley advocated a catholic spirit, evidenced in evangelical ecumenicity that extended not only to George Whitefield, but to all in the Calvinist camp as well. Thus, it was John Wesley writing on a very personal level who said:

The differences which begin in points of opinion seldom terminate there. They generally spread into the affections, and then separate chief friends. Nor are any animosities so deep and irreconcilable as those that spring from disagreement in religion. For this cause the bitterest enemies of a man are those of his own household . . . It is therefore nothing more than we may expect if those who differ from us either in religious opinions or practice soon contract a sharpness, yea, bitterness toward us; if they are more and more prejudiced against us, till they conceive as ill an opinion of our persons as of our principles.[117]

Wesley continued by noting that if positive results for the Kingdom of God are seen in the ministry of one of differing opinions, fellow believers were not to forbid that one from continuing the work. "Suppose then a man have no intercourse with us, suppose he be not of our party, suppose he separate from our Church, yea, and widely differ from us both in judgment, practice, and affection; yet if we see even this man 'casting out devils' Jesus saith, 'Forbid him not.'"[118] Those that attempt to prevent such ministry from continuing are guilty of bigotry, which Wesley defined as "too strong an attachment to, or fondness for, our own party, opinion, Church, and religion. Therefore he is a bigot who is so fond of any of these, so strongly attached to them, as to forbid any who casts out devils, because he differs from himself in any or all these particulars."[119] Proof of one being able to "cast out devils" (i.e. effectively leading someone to saving faith in Christ) was easily discerned:

Is there full proof, first, that a person before us was a gross, open sinner? Secondly, that he is not so now; that he has broke off his sins, and
lives a Christian life? And thirdly, that his change was wrought by his
hearing this man preach? If these three points be plain and undeniable,
then you have sufficient, reasonable proof, such as you cannot resist
without wilful sin, that this man casts out devils.[120]

Wesley's final advice was that of Calvin's to Bullinger, "Let Luther call me an
hundred devils; I will still reverence him as a messenger of God."[121]
    A second sermon first released in 1750, was Wesley's most complete state-
ment of his belief in the importance of possessing a catholic spirit. In every
statement of what he considered to be "Christian essentials," Wesley's "concern
is to narrow the field of irreducible disagreement between professing, practicing
Christians and to transfer their concerns from argument about faith in Christ to
faith itself and to its consequences."[122] For Wesley, the propagation of a catholic
spirit could be reduced to one simple question:

Every wise man therefore will allow others the same liberty of thinking
which he desires they should allow him; and will no more insist on
their embracing his opinions than he would have them insist on his embracing theirs. He bears with those who differ from him, and only asks
him with whom he desires to unite in love that single question. "Is thine
heart right, as my heart is with thy heart?"[123]

Wesley continued by first defining what he meant by a "right heart." One
whose heart is right: believes in a loving, active God; believes Jesus to be the
Son of God and as the one offered for the sins of the world; loves God with
one's whole being; is employed in doing the will of God; serves God with the
proper attitude of fear; loves one's neighbor as oneself; and shows that love in
good works.[124] These were basics upon which all in the evangelical camp could
agree. There was no mention of doctrinaire ideals, only the essence of true,
scriptural Christianity as Wesley viewed it. Wesley concluded this section by
stating, "If thou art thus minded, may every Christian say — yea, if thou art but
sincerely desirous of it, and following on till thou attain — then 'thy heart is
right, as my heart is with thy heart.'"[125]
    This was not to suggest that one thus minded needed to accept the rest of
Wesley's theology. Nor did it mean that there needed to be agreement on less-
vital doctrine. Worship styles did not have to be brought to unanimity. Wesley
urged, "Keep you your opinion, I mine; and that as steadily as ever. You need
not even endeavor to come over to me, or bring me over to you. I do not desire
you to dispute those points, or to hear or speak one word concerning them. Let
all opinions alone on one side and the other. Only 'give me thine hand.'"[126]
Those who could agree with Wesley on these terms were encouraged by him to

exhibit their catholic spirit by loving those who differed "with a very tender affection, as a friend that is closer than a brother;" by loving with a self-giving attitude; by praying for God to "speedily correct what he sees amiss and supply what is wanting;" by encouraging each other "to love and to good works;" and by loving, not only in word, but in deed, namely, by joining together to do the work of the Kingdom of God."[127] Wesley determined not only to encourage others to put these principles into practice, but was prepared to put them into practice himself.

Wesley foresaw the accusations that would be lodged against him. He would not leave himself open to charges of Latitudinarianism and theological indifference. Wesley was not advocating an ecumenism that stretched to all who claimed to be Christian. Wesley advocated instead an ecumenism that was evangelically based: based on the foundational principles to which all warm-hearted proponents of experiential faith could subscribe, whether a member of the Roman Catholic Church, the Church of England, or any number of Dissenting bodies. The person of a truly catholic spirit would remain committed to his or her denomination:

> But while he is steadily fixed in his religious principles, in what he believes to be the truth as it is in Jesus; while he firmly adheres to that worship of God which he judges to be most acceptable in his sight; and while he is united by the tenderest and closest ties to one particular congregation; his heart is enlarged toward all mankind, those he knows and those he does not; he embraces with strong and cordial affection neighbors and strangers, friends and enemies. This is catholic or universal love. And he that has this is of a catholic spirit. For love alone gives the title to this character — catholic love is a catholic spirit.[128]

Wesley concluded:

> If then we take this word in the strictest sense, a man of a catholic spirit is one who in the manner above mentioned "gives his hand" to all whose "hearts are right with his heart." One who knows how to value and praise God for all the advantages he enjoys: with regard to the knowledge of the things of God, the true, scriptural manner of worshipping him; and above all his union with a congregation fearing God and working righteousness. One who, retaining these blessings with the strictest care, keeping them as the apple of his eye, at the same time loves as friends, brethren in the Lord, as members of Christ and children of God, as joint partakers now of the present kingdom of God, and fellow-heirs of his eternal Kingdom, all of whatever opinion or worship

or congregation who believe in the Lord Jesus Christ; who love God and man; who, rejoicing to please and fearing to offend God, are careful to abstain from evil and zealous of good works. He is the man of a truly catholic spirit who bears all these continually upon his heart, who having an unspeakable tenderness for their persons, and longing for their welfare, does not cease to commend them to God in prayer, as well as to plead their cause before men; who speaks comfortably to them, and labors by all his words to strengthen their hands in God. He assists them to the uttermost of his power in all things, spiritual and temporal. He is ready "to spend and be spent for them;" yea, "to lay down his life for" their sake.[129]

According to Wesley, a catholic spirit was not easy to cultivate, yet the fruit of a catholic spirit was well worth the effort. The results for Wesley included a Methodist movement that, while possessing certain doctrinal distinctives, allowed space for theological inquiry and a "big tent" for like-minded individuals from any denomination, and, as important, a friendship that neither doctrine nor death could destroy.

Conclusion

Whitefield never understood Wesley's brand of Arminianism, while Wesley at least strove to understand Whitefield's Calvinism. For Whitefield, there was only one type of Arminianism, and in his mind, it made humanity at least partially responsible for its salvation. Such was not the Arminianism of John Wesley. Whitefield wrote, "Man is nothing: he hath a free will to go to hell, but none to go to heaven, till God worketh in him to will and to do after his good pleasure. It is God must prevent, God must accompany, God must follow with his grace, or Jesus Christ will bleed in vain."[130] Wesley would have had little disagreement with Whitefield's letter. Humanity, without the grace of God, was doomed to eternal punishment. But God, out of divine mercy, has offered his prevenient grace to all humanity whereby one is enabled "to choose further to cooperate with saving grace. By offering the will the restored capacity to respond to grace, the person then may freely and increasingly become an active, willing participant in receiving the conditions for justification."[131] God, indeed, must prevent, accompany and follow his grace. As Randy Maddox has argued:

> Wesley's consuming emphasis on the deity of Christ was an expression of his conviction that *God is the one who takes initiative in our salvation*: it is God who died in Christ to make possible our pardon; it is God who awakens us to our need of grace in Christ the Prophet and drives us to Christ the Priest; it is God who initiates our restored rela-

tionship in Christ the Priest; and, it is God who guides us as Christ the King, leading us into all holiness and happiness.[132]

This is a further indication that the apparent theological differences between Whitefield and Wesley were more a matter of emphasis rather than complete disagreement. Whitefield endeavored to protect the sovereignty of God. Wesley, while not denying God's sovereignty, fought to protect human freedom of choice with which God in his sovereignty had endowed humanity. This is the key factor in understanding the strained relationship and in comprehending the relative ease with which they reunited. Indeed, Wesley could have exhibited more restraint and not printed his sermon against predestination and waited until Whitefield was back in England in an attempt to work out an amicable agreement to disagree. Yet for Whitefield to write that he had not publicly supported election prior to 1740 was audacious, to say the least. But both men were attempting to defend the integrity of their respective theological systems.

Here again, the personalities of the two came into play. Whitefield, the dramatic evangelist, believed he must protect the integrity of the revival that he saw as being carried on largely by Calvinistic preaching. From a North American perspective, the generalization was valid. Whitefield attacked Wesley's Arminianism on the basis that "all" Arminians seek to make humans, in some way, saviors of themselves. While setting out to accomplish an honorable deed, Whitefield made the mistake of categorizing all Arminians as one and the same. Whitefield either did not understand or did not seek to understand the integrity of Wesley's system. Wesley was no Pelagian! Human beings could not save themselves. But Wesley believed that through prevenient grace, God had gifted all humanity with the ability to respond to the gospel message. Where Wesley believed all had access to the faith whereby they could respond, Whitefield believed that only certain chosen ones had been given the opportunity.

Wesley's personality was indeed pastoral, while his mind was actively engaged in defending his theological system against competing theologies. Even his sermon *Free Grace* is a careful examination of the logical deficiencies in the Calvinistic system as he saw them. His sermon was designed both to instruct his hearers in the truth and also to destruct the poorly constructed arguments of the Calvinists. If the system had been logically defensible in Wesley's mind, *Free Grace* may never have been preached nor printed. But for Wesley, the only system that met the demands of the sanctified rational mind was Arminianism, which taught that the sovereign God, in his love for humanity, has made salvation accessible to all, though not all will respond to his merciful invitation.

Whitefield and Wesley maintained a warm friendship until Whitefield died in 1770. Whitefield never fully accepted Wesley's Arminianism, nor did Wesley fully accept Whitefield's Calvinism. Yet both realized that the message that they preached, the necessity of experiential faith in an individual's life, was more than enough basis for a cordial working and personal relationship. They preached the same gospel: humanity is utterly depraved, helpless in and of itself to do anything about the situation. God, in his infinite mercy, had intervened, and declared that those who believed in the atoning sacrifice of Jesus Christ would be saved. Forgiveness and eternal life in the presence of God were the present and future realities for those who accepted the message. The theological nuances related to these basic truths became incidental.

In the broader context of Arminian/Calvinist relations, Wesley met with Howell Harris in 1747, and both Wesley and Harris, along with Whitefield, agreed to circulate the *Minutes* of their Conferences. In the early 1760s, Wesley, Whitefield, and Selina, Countess of Huntingdon, continued negotiations and generally agreed to respect each other's ministries. The decade of the 1760s was marked by growing cooperation.[133] Perhaps A. Skevington Wood has summarized this best: the "fire and force" of the English revival did not rest in Calvinism or Arminianism but in what both groups held in common, namely that salvation comes through Jesus Christ.[134]

Unfortunately, after Whitefield's death, the doctrinal distinctives of the two camps once again took center stage in the drama of Methodism. The Calvinistic Controversy, which began in 1770 forever divided English evangelicalism into at least a two-party system. Wesley's personality alone was not enough to keep the two sides together. No Calvinistic leader arose that shared Whitefield's common goal with Wesley of an evangelical ecumenical movement.

George Whitefield and John Wesley could ultimately consider each other "a brother," along with countless others who disagreed with them on matters of opinion. They could consider those of differing opinions as brothers and sisters because theirs was "a religion of the heart," that which Ted Campbell concludes was "the basis or 'bottom' of all religion in the Evangelical Revival of eighteenth-century Britain."[135]

Perhaps no one could better state the importance of the relationship of John Wesley and George Whitefield to the Evangelical Revival than one who knew them both, and in fact may have been a major contributor to their crisis of friendship. Charles Wesley, John's closest brother and co-laborer, was instrumental in Whitefield's conversion to experiential Christianity. Yet it was also Charles, who in 1741, published his *Hymns on God's Everlasting Love*, which included two highly polemical hymns, "The Cry of the Reprobate," and "The Horrible Decree." A later edition included the hymn "The Lord's Controversy," where "the ministers of true religion struggle against the (Calvinistic) priests of Moloch."[136] But it was the same Charles Wesley who penned the ultimate description of the importance of evangelical ecumenicity to the future of the revival:

Ah! wherefore did we ever seem to part,
Or clash in sentiment, while one in heart?
What dire device did the old serpent find,
To put asunder those whom God had joined?
From folly and self-love opinion rose,
To sever friends who never yet were foes;
To baffle and divert our noblest aim,

Confound our pride, and cover us with shame;
To make us blush beneath her short-lived pow'r,
And glad the world with one triumphant hour.
But lo! the snare is broke, the captive's freed,
By faith on all the hostile powers we tread,
And crush through Jesus' strength the serpent's head,

One in his hand, oh, may we still remain,
Fast bound with love's indissoluble chain;
His love the tie that binds us to his throne,
His love the bond that perfects us in one;
His love (let all the ground of friendship see)
His only love constrains our hearts t' agree,
And gives the rivet for eternity. [137]

The continuation of this evangelical ecumenism was much more important than doctrinal differences, personality issues, and matters of self-promotion. Once Whitefield and Wesley realized this, not only the revival, but their friendship could move forward. They have left a paradigm to the contemporary evangelical Church. Much more important than what keeps evangelicals apart, is what should hold them together: the fundamental teaching of the necessity of experiential, warm-hearted Christianity. Further, evangelicals can find in Wesley and Whitefield a paradigm for looking beyond evangelical denominations in a concerted effort to find "experiential religion" in traditions historically different from their own.

This was not a call to abandon the integrity of one's theological system. Neither Wesley nor Whitefield sacrificed the integrity of their respective systems. They were willing, however, to recognize "the religion of the heart" wherever they discovered it. Evangelicals should value and celebrate warm-hearted Christianity wherever they find it as well. Then the Church can lift its unified voice in prayer to the Lord of the Church, as did John Wesley, "Would to God that all the party names and unscriptural phrases and forms which have divided the Christian world were forgot, and that we might all agree to sit down together as humble, loving disciples at the feet of our common Master, to hear his words, to imbibe his Spirit, and to transcribe his life in our own."[138] Then may the Church sing with Charles Wesley:

> Come on, my Whitefield! (since the strife is past,
> And friends at first are friends again at last)
> Our hands, our hearts, and counsels let us join
> In mutual league, t'advance the work divine,
> Our one contention now, our single aim,
> To pluck poor souls as brands out of the flame;
> To spread the victory of that bloody cross,
> And gasp our latest breath in the Redeemer's cause.[139]

The quest for evangelical ecumenicity (or evangelical catholicity?) did not see complete fulfillment in eighteenth-century British Methodism. Arminian Methodism would continue to grow and spread, seeing advance both in England and in the former British colonies in North America. Evangelical Calvinism would know similar growth. While these two streams of English revivalism went their separate ways, two of their leaders have left a legacy for their descendants, illustrating how the quest for evangelical ecumenicity can be successful by downplaying agendas, overlooking differences in "non-essentials," and focusing on the vitally important fundamentals of experiential Christianity. By following their example, perhaps the diverse sectors of the Church will realize that they differ from one another by only a "hair's breadth."

Notes

1. Randy L. Maddox, "Opinion, Religion and *Catholic Spirit*: John Wesley on Theological Integrity." *Asbury Theological Journal* 47 (1992): 79.

2. Ibid., 76-77.

3. "Whitefield based his qualifications for proclaiming the necessity of the new birth on his acquaintance with 'experimental religion' not his mastery of prescribed theology. He linked his message to the personal experience of the messenger, filtering the message of the new birth through his own intense conversion." Frank Lambert, "The Great Awakening as Artifact: George Whitefield and the Construction of Intercolonial Revival, 1739-1745," *Church History* 60, no. 2 (1991): 223-246.

4. Whitefield, *Letters*, 182.

5. Ibid., 205.

6. Ibid., 575. Whitefield writes, "This (election) is the established doctrine of scripture, and acknowledged as such in the 17th article of the church of England, as Bishop Burnet himself confesses; yet dear Mr. Wesley absolutely denies it."

7. Coppedge, 174.

8. Whitefield, *Journals*, 13.

9. Ibid., 510.

10. Stout, 64.

11. Whitefield, *Journals*, 154.

12. Whitefield, *Letters*, 216. Letter CCXXV.

13. Ibid., 222. Letter CCXXXII.

14. Lambert, 239. Lambert lists the North American recipients of Whitefield's letters: James Habersham and Jonathan Barber in Georgia, Josiah Smith, Isaac Chanler, and Hugh Bryan in Charleston, Benjamin Franklin, Samuel Finley, and James Blair in Philadelphia, Gilbert and William Tennent in New Jersey, Ebenezer Pemberton and James Noble in New York, Benjamin Colman and William Cooper in Boston, and Jonathan Parsons in Connecticut.

15. Whitefield, *Letters*, 152-153. Letter CLXV. Written to the Rev. Mr. J., who is not identified.

16. Ibid., 202. Letter CCXI.

17. Lambert, 233.

18. Ibid., 239.

19. Ward, 8.

20. Lambert, 234.

21. Ibid., 234.

22. Stout, 95.

23. Lambert, 237. Seward and Bolton's press was carried out in the pages of the *Pennsylvania Gazette*, while no less a figure than Charles Chauncy made the argument for why the opposition clergy in Boston refrained from attacking Whitefield.

24. Ibid., 245.

25. Ibid., 244.

26. Benjamin Franklin, *Autobiography* (New York: Pocket Books, Inc., nd), 134.

27. Ibid., 134.

28. Whitefield, *Journals*, 39.

29. Stout, 13.

30. Pemberton was the pastor of the First Presbyterian Church of New York City from 1727 to 1753. He was a close associate of Rev. Joseph Sewell, a Commissioner of the Society for the Propagation of the Gospel in New England and Parts Adjacent, and both were dedicated supporters of the revivals. Whitefield, *Journals*, 528.

31. Whitefield, *Letters*, 122-123. Letter CXXX, written November 28, 1739.

32. Ibid., 134. Letter CXLIV, dated December 8, 1739.

33. Charles Wallace, Jr., ed., *Susanna Wesley: The Complete Writings* (New York: Oxford University Press, 1997), 467.

34. Ibid., 466.

35. Lambert, 233.

36. Ibid., 232. Lambert notes that Whitefield "made his success a central theme of his message. Whitefield attributed his success to both invisible, inward manifestations of God's special calling and to visible, outward signs evidenced by numerous listeners." He often spoke of "uncommon manifestations granted (him) from above" and of being "overpowered with a sense of God's infinite majesty."

37. Whitefield, *Letters*, 499. Letter XVI.

38. Ibid., 156. Letter CLXIX, dated March 26, 1740, from Savannah.

39. Ibid., 185. Letter CXCIV.

40. Ibid., 156.

41. Ibid., 182.

42. Ibid., 189.

43. Whitefield, *Journals*. Whitefield's sixth *Journal*, covering the period from January 1740 until June of the same year, highlights numerous encounters with clergy of Calvinistic tendencies.

44. Ibid., 401.

45. Ibid., 403. One of Whitefield's favorite themes was the imputed righteousness of Christ to the believer's life, another key Calvinistic belief. It seems odd that seekers would be interested in such a doctrine had it not been recently preached and affirmed.

46. Ibid., 420.

47. George Whitefield, *The Lord our Righteousness: A Sermon preached on Fryday forenone, September 11th 1741. In the High-Church-Yard of Glasgow, upon Jer. xxxiii. 16. / By the Reverend George Whitefield, taken from his own mouth, and published at the earnest desire of many of the hearers. And since revised and corrected.* (Worcester: American Antiquarian Society, 1955-1983), micropaque.

48. Whitefield, *Select Sermons*, 116.

49. Ibid., 121.

50. Ibid., 129.

51. George Whitefield, *Sermons on Various Subjects* (Philadelphia: B. Franklin, 1740), micropaque.

52. George Whitefield, *The Works of the Reverend George Whitefield* (London: E. and C. Dilly, 1771-1772), microform.

53. Ibid. Italics added.

54. Ibid. Without doubt, this sermon had been preached, not solely published, prior to the letters of the spring and summer of 1740. An earlier edition was published in Philadelphia by Andrew and William Bradford in 1739. George Whitefield, *What Think ye of Christ?: A sermon preached at Kennington-Common, near London, and at Philadelphia, 1739* (Philadelphia: Andrew and William Bradford, 1739), micropaque.

55. Ibid. Whitefield is expounding on Romans 5:19, "For as by one man's disobedience many were made sinners, so also by one man's obedience many will be made righteous."

56. Whitefield, *Letters*, 206. Letter CCXV, posted to Mrs. J. L. in Bristol on August 26, 1740.

57. Ibid., 101. Letter CVI, probably written to the Rev. John Hutton.

58. Gillies, 478.

59. Ibid., 417. From the sermon "The Power of Christ's Resurrection."

60. Whitefield, *Journals*, 62. According to Whitefield's memory, he came to this conclusion as early as 1735, a full three years before the Wesley brothers came to the same conclusion.

61. Ibid., 109.

62. Ibid., 148.

63. Whitefield, *Letters*, 87. Letter XCI, dated November 10, 1739, from Philadelphia.

64. Outler, ed., *Sermons, Vol. 2*, 343.

65. Ibid., 343.

66. Davies, *Works, Vol. 9*, 35.

67. Ibid., 35.

68. Ibid., 41.

69. Ibid., 41.

70. Howe O. Thomas, Jr., "John Wesley's Understanding of the Theological Distinction Between 'Essentials' and 'Opinions,'" *Methodist History* 26 (January 1988), 142.

71. Maddox, "Opinion, Religion, and *Catholic Spirit*," 76.

72. Thomas, 143.

73. Maddox, "Opinion, Religion and *Catholic Spirit*," 76.

74. Thomas, 144.

75. Ibid., 145.

76. Cragg, 23.

77. Davies, 254-255.

78. Ibid., 34. Written in Wesley's *The Character of a Methodist*.

79. Outler, *Sermons, Vol. 2*, 344.

80. Whitefield, *Letters*, 33. Letter XXX, assumedly written to James Hutton.

81. Ibid., 58. Letter LVIII, to an unnamed recipient.

82. Ibid., 115. Letter CXX to an unnamed recipient.

83. Ibid.,126. Letter CXXXV. Apparently Whitefield's "one question" could be expressed in at least three different ways.

84. Ibid., 142. Letter CLII.

85. Ibid., 484, 486. These references are found in two letters, the earliest from the summer of 1735, the latter from September 1736.

86. Ibid., 495. Whitefield signs the letters, "Your dutiful son and servant," and "Your unworthy son and servant," respectively.

87. Ibid., 497-498. Letter 15.

88. Ibid., 499. Interestingly, after encouraging Wesley to "keep in" the sermon *Free Grace*, Whitefield bemoans the fact that Wesley has "cast a lot" seeking divine guidance on the question of going public with the sermon. Wesley's practice of casting lots was attacked by Whitefield in more detail in his response to *Free Grace*, noting, "I have often questioned, as I do now, whether in so doing, you did not tempt the Lord. A due exercise of religious prudence, without a lot, would have directed you in that matter." (Whitefield, *Journals*, 572.) Yet on at least one occasion, earlier in 1739, Whitefield had used a lot to determine divine guidance. On January 5, Whitefield met at Islington with "seven true ministers of Jesus Christ." On matters upon which they were in doubt, "after prayer, we determined by lot." Whitefield left that meeting "with a full conviction that God was going to do great things among us." (Ibid., 196.) Commentators on Whitefield's life typically overlook the fact that Whitefield, too, resorted to this practice.

89. Susan F. Harrington, "Friendship Under Fire: George Whitefield and John Wesley, 1739-1741," *Andover Newton Quarterly* 15 (1975): 171-172. Whitefield wrote to Wesley on March 26, May 24, and June 25. Wesley responded to the May 24 letter on August 9. Whitefield wrote again on August 25 and September 25, an apparent answer to a lost letter of Wesley's dated March 25. Whitefield would write again on November 9 and 24, and post his response to Wesley's sermon on December 24, in answer to the August 9 letter.

90. Baker, ed., *Letters of John Wesley, Vol. 26*, 31.

91. Whitefield. *Letters*, 219. Letter CCXXIX.

92. Frank Baker, "Whitefield's Break with the Wesleys," *Church Quarterly*. 3 (1970), 108.

93. Whitefield. *Letters*, 225. Letter CCXXXVI.

94. The complete letter is published in: Whitefield, *Journals*, 571-588.

95. Stuart Henry and Luke Tyerman held that the letter Wesley received and tore up on February 1 was Whitefield's dated September 25. But as Susan Harrington pointed out, this letter lacks the impact that would have convinced Wesley of the necessity to destroy it. Far more likely is the view held by Harrington (p. 80), and also by N. Curnock, John Telford, and more recently by Frank Baker ("Whitefield's Break with the Wesleys," 109), and Richard Heitzenrater (*Wesley and the People Called Methodists*, 121).

96. Ward and Heitzenrater, *Journal and Diaries, Vol. 19*, 188-189.

97. Ibid., 189-190.

98. Whitefield, *Letters*, 331. Letter CCCLXIII.

99. Ibid., 341-342. Letter CCCLXXIV.

100. Ibid., 357. Letter CCCLXXXV.

101. Ibid., 372. Letter CCCXCIX.

102. Ward and Heitzenrater, *Journal and Diaries, Vol. 19*, 260.

103. Ibid., 332-333.

104. Cragg, 173.

105. Ward and Heitzenrater, *Journal and Diaries, Vol. 20*, 318-319.

106. Ward and Heitzenrater, *Journal and Diaries, Vol. 21*, 33.

107. Ward and Heitzenrater, *Journal and Diaries, Vol. 22*, 28-29.

108. John Wesley, *Works, Vol. XII*, 272. Letter CCXXXV, dated December 6, 1767.

109. Whitefield, *Letters*, 306. Letter CCCXXXVIII.

110. Ibid., 434-435. Letter CCCCLIII.

111. Ibid., 438. Letter CCCCLVI.

112. Ibid., 515. Letter 33, written August 17, 1742 to the Rev. Mr. John Willison of Dundee.

113. Bready, 425.

114. The sermon text is Mark 9:38-39, "And John answered him, saying, Master, we saw one casting out devils in thy name, and we forbade him, because he followeth not us. And Jesus said, Forbid him not."

115. Outler, ed., *Sermons, Vol. 2*, 69-70.

116. Ibid., 70.

117. Ibid., 72.

118. Ibid., 72-73.

119. Ibid., 76.

120. Ibid., 73.

121. Ibid., 78. Wesley prefaced his quotation from Calvin with the parenthesis, "O that he had always breathed the same spirit!" Considering the previous statement Wesley had made concerning those who differed over the doctrines that separated Arminians and Calvinists, perhaps Wesley even had Whitefield (or himself!) in mind when quoting Calvin.

122. Ibid., 79. This is Outler's own assessment of Wesley in his introduction to Wesley's sermon *Catholic Spirit*.

123. Ibid., 85. The question comes from an obscure passage in 2 Kings 10:15.

124. Ibid., 87-89.

125. Ibid., 89.

126. Ibid., 89.

127. Ibid., 90-92.

128. Ibid., 94.

129. Ibid., 95.

130. Whitefield, *Letters*, 90. Letter XCIV dated November 10, 1739.

131. Oden, 243.

132. Maddox, *Responsible Grace*, 117-118.

133. Campbell, 127.

134. A. Skevington Wood, *The Inextinguishable Blaze* (Grand Rapids: Eerdmans Publishing Co., 1960), 232.

135. Campbell, 99.

136. John R. Tyson, "God's Everlasting Love: Charles Wesley and the Predestinarian Controversy," *Evangelical Journal* 3 (Fall 1985): 58. Tyson quips, "It is small wonder that George Whitefield, the preacher of Calvinistic Methodism, disapproved of these hymns."

137. Arnold A. Dallimore, *A Heart Set Free: The Life of Charles Wesley* (Westchester, IL: Crossway Books, 1988), 230-231. From *An Epistle to the Rev. George Whitefield.*

138. John Wesley, *Notes on the Bible*, 402. Quoted in: Douglas Jacobsen, "Purity or Tolerance: The Social Dimension of Hermeneutics in the Calvinist, Arminian and American Evangelical Traditions," *Evangelical Journal* 11 (1993): 19.

139. Jacobsen, 191.

List of Sources

Primary Sources

Baker, Frank, ed. *The Works of John Wesley, Vol. 25-26: Letters.* Oxford: Clarendon Press, 1980-1982.

Beckerlegge, Oliver A., and Franz Hildebrandt, eds. *The Works of John Wesley, Vol. 7: A Collection of Hymns for the use of the People Called Methodist.* Oxford: Clarendon Press, 1987.

Bray, Gerald, ed. *Documents of the English Reformation.* Minneapolis: Fortress Press, 1994.

Buckland, A.R., ed. *Selected Sermons of George Whitefield.* Philadelphia: The Union Press, 1904.

Cragg, Gerald R., ed. *The Works of John Wesley, Vol. 11: The Appeals to Men of Reason and Religion and Certain Related Open Letters.* Oxford: Clarendon Press, 1975.

Davies, Rupert E., ed. *The Works of John Wesley, Vol. 9: The Methodist Societies; History, Nature, and Design.* Nashville: Abingdon Press, 1989.

Defoe, Daniel. *A Tour Through the Whole Island of Great Britain.* Middlesex, UK: Penguin Books, Ltd., 1971.

Fant, Clyde E., Jr., and William M. Pinson, Jr., eds. *20 Centuries of Great Preaching, Vol. 3: Wesley to Finney (1703-1875).* Waco, TX: Word Books, 1971.

Franklin, Benjamin. *Autobiography.* New York: Pocket Books, Inc., nd.

Outler, Albert C., ed. *The Works of John Wesley, Vol. 1-4: Sermons.* Nashville: Abingdon Press, 1985.

Wallace, Charles, Jr., ed. *Susanna Wesley: The Complete Writings.* New York: Oxford University Press, 1997.

Ward, W. Reginald, and Richard P. Heitzenrater, eds. *The Works of John Wesley, Vol. 18-23: Journal and Diaries.* Nashville: Abingdon Press, 1988-1995.

Wesley, John. *Notes on the Bible.* Grand Rapids: Francis Asbury Press, 1987.

———. *Works.* Peabody, MA: Hendrickson Publishing Co., 1991.

Whaling, Frank, ed. *John and Charles Wesley: Selected Writings and Hymns.* New York: Paulist Press, 1981.

Whitefield, George. *Journals.* Carlisle, PA: Banner of Truth Trust, 1992.

———. *Letters, 1734-1742.* Carlisle, PA: Banner of Truth Trust, 1976.

———. *Select Sermons of George Whitefield.* Carlisle, PA: Banner of Truth Trust, 1990.

———. *Sermons on Various Subjects.* Philadelphia: B. Franklin, 1740 (microform).

———. *The Lord our Righteousness: A Sermon preached on Fryday forenoon, September 11 1741. In the High-Church-Yard of Glasgow, upon*

Jer. xxxiii. 16./ By the Reverend Mr. George Whitefield, taken from his own mouth, and published at the earnest desire of many of the hearers. And since revised and corrected. Boston: S. Kneeland and T. Green, 1742 (microform).

————. *The Works of the Reverend George Whitefield.* London: E. and C. Dilly, 1771-1772 (microform).

Secondary Sources

Bicknell, E. J. *A Theological Introduction to the Thirty-Nine Articles of the Church of England.* London: Longmans, Green, and Co., 1961.

Black, Jeremy, ed. *British Politics and Society from Walpole to Pitt, 1742-1789.* London: Macmillan Education Ltd., 1990.

Bready, J. Wesley. *England Before and After Wesley.* London: Hodder and Stoughton, 1938.

Browne, Edward Harold. *An Exposition of the Thirty-Nine Articles: Historical and Doctrinal.* London: Longmans, Green, and Co., 1865.

Burrows, Aelred. "Wesley, the Catholic." In *John Wesley: Contemporary Perspectives.* Edited by John Stacey. London: Epworth Press, 1988.

Campbell, Ted A. *John Wesley and Christian Antiquity: Religious Vision and Cultural Changes.* Nashville: Kingswood Books, 1991.

————. *The Religion of the Heart: A Study of European Religious Life in the Seventeenth and Eighteenth Centuries.* Columbia, SC: University of South Carolina Press, 1991.

Cashin, Edward J. *Beloved Bethesda: A History of George Whitefield's Home for Boys, 1740-2000.* Macon, GA: Mercer University Press, 2001.

Cheyney, Edward P. *Modern English Reform: From Individualism to Socialism.* New York: A.S. Barnes and Company, 1962.

Clark, J.C.D. *English Society, 1688-1832.* Cambridge: Cambridge University Press, 1986.

Collins, Kenneth J. *The Scripture Way of Salvation: The Heart of John Wesley's Theology.* Nashville: Abingdon Press, 1997.

Coppedge, Allan. *John Wesley in Theological Debate.* Wilmore, KY: Wesley Heritage Press, 1987.

Dallimore, Arnold A. *A Heart Set Free: The Life of Charles Wesley.* Westchester, IL: Crossway Books, 1988.

————. *George Whitefield: God's Anointed Servant in the Great Revival of the Eighteenth Century.* Wheaton, IL: Crossway Books, 1990.

————. *George Whitefield: The Life and Times of the Great Evangelist of the Eighteenth-Century Revival, Vol. 1 & 2.* London: Banner of Truth Trust, 1970-1980.

Davies, Rupert, and Gordon Rupp. *A History of the Methodist Church in Great Britain.* London: Epworth Press, 1965.

Fackre, Gabriel. *Ecumenical Faith in Evangelical Perspective.* Grand Rapids: Eerdmans Publishing Co., 1993.

Gillies, John. *Memoirs of Rev. George Whitefield.* Hartford, CT: Edwin Hunt, 1843.

Gonzalez, Justo L. *The Story of Christianity, Vol. 2: The Reformation to the Present Day.* San Francisco: Harper & Row, 1992.

Gunter, W. Stephen. *The Limits of "Love Divine."* Nashville: Kingswood Books, 1989.

Hattersley, Roy. *The Life of John Wesley: A Brand from the Burning.* New York: Doubleday, 2003.

Heitzenrater, Richard P. *Wesley and the People Called Methodists.* Nashville: Abingdon Press, 1995.

Henry, Stuart Clark. *George Whitefield: Wayfaring Witness.* Nashville: Abingdon Press, 1957.

Hildebrandt, Franz. *Christianity According to the Wesleys.* London: Epworth Press, 1956.

Hynson, Leon O. *To Reform the Nation: Theological Foundations of Wesley's Ethics.* Grand Rapids: Francis Asbury Press, 1984.

Keefer, Luke L., Jr. "John Wesley: Disciple of Early Christianity." Ph.D. diss., Temple University, 1982.

Knox, Ronald. *Enthusiasm: A Chapter in the History of Religion with Special Reference to the Seventeenth and Eighteenth Centuries.* New York: Oxford University Press, 1961.

Lindstrom, Harald. *Wesley and Sanctification: A Study in the Doctrine of Salvation.* Grand Rapids: Francis Asbury Press, 1980.

MacLear, G.F. *An Introduction to the Articles of the Church of England.* London: Macmillan and Co., 1895.

Maddox, Randy L. *Responsible Grace: John Wesley's Practical Theology.* Nashville: Kingswood Books, 1994.

Methodist Preacher. *John Wesley the Methodist: A Plain Account of His Life and Work.* New York: Methodist Book Concern, 1903.

Monk, Robert C. *A Study of the Christian Life: John Wesley, His Puritan Heritage.* London: Epworth Press, 1966.

Moorman, J.R.H. *A History of the Church in England.* London: A.C. Black, 1986.

Morgan, Kenneth O., ed. *The Oxford History of Britain.* Oxford: Oxford University Press, 1988.

Noll, Mark A. *A History of Christianity in the United States and Canada.* Grand Rapids: Eerdmans Publishing Co., 1992.

Nuttall, Geoffrey F. "Continental Pietism and the Evangelical Movement in Britain." In *Pietismus und Reveil*, ed. By J. van den Berg, Leiden: E.J. Brill, 1978.

Oden, Thomas C. *John Wesley's Scriptural Christianity.* Grand Rapids: Zondervan Publishing House, 1994.

Outler, Albert, ed. *John Wesley.* New York: Oxford University Press, 1980.

Paulson, Ross. "On the Meaning of Faith in the Great Awakening and the Methodist Revival." In *The Immigration of Ideas*, by O.F. Ander, J.I. Dowie, and J.T. Tredway, Rock Island, IL: Augustana Historical Society, 1968.

Piette, Maximin. *John Wesley in the Evolution of Protestantism.* New York: Sheed and Ward, 1979.

Porter, George Roy. *English Society in the Eighteenth Century.* Hammondsworth, UK: Penguin Books, 1982.

Rack, Henry D. *Reasonable Enthusiast: John Wesley and the Rise of Methodism.* Nashville: Abingdon Press, 1992.

Rowe, Kenneth E., ed. *The Place of John Wesley in the Christian Tradition: Essays delivered at Drew University in celebration of the commencement of the publication of the Oxford Edition of the Works of John Wesley.* Metuchen, NJ: Scarecrow Press, 1976.

Rupp, Ernest Gordon. *Religion in England.* Oxford: Clarendon Press, 1986.

Solomon, Robert C. and Kathleen M. Higgins. *A Short History of Philosophy.* New York: Oxford University Press, 1996.

Smith, Timothy L. *Whitefield and Wesley on the New Birth.* Grand Rapids: Eerdmans Publishing Co., 1986.

Sommerville, C. John. *The Secularization of Early Modern England: From Religious Culture to Religious Faith.* New York: Oxford University Press, 1992.

Stephen, Sir Leslie. *History of English Thought in the Eighteenth Century, Vol. 1.* New York: Harbinger Books, 1962.

Stout, Harry S. *The Divine Dramatist: George Whitefield and the Rise of Modern Evangelicalism.* Grand Rapids: Eerdmans Publishing Co., 1991.

Todd, John M. *John Wesley and the Catholic Church.* London: Hodder and Stoughton, 1958.

Towlson, Clifford W. *Moravian and Methodist: Relationships and Influences in the Eighteenth Century.* London: Epworth Press, 1957.

Trevelyan, George Macaulay. *History of England.* New York: Longmans, Green, and Co., 1928.

Tyson, John R., ed. *Charles Wesley: A Reader.* New York: Oxford University Press, 1989.

Walsh, John, Colin Haydon, and Stephen Taylor, eds. *The Church of England c. 1689-c. 1833: From Toleration to Tractarianiam.* Cambridge: Cambridge University Press, 1993.

Ward, William R. *The Protestant Evangelical Awakening.* New York: Cambridge University Press, 1992.

Williams, Colin. *John Wesley's Theology Today.* Nashville: Abingdon Press, 1964.

Wood, A. Skevington. *The Burning Heart.* Minneapolis: Bethany Fellowship Inc., 1978.

Journal Articles

Baker, Frank. "The Origins, Character, and Influence of John Wesley's *Thoughts upon Slavery.*" *Methodist History* 22 (1984): 75-86.

————. "Whitefield's Break with the Wesleys." *Church Quarterly* 3 (1970): 103-113.

Brantley, Richard E. "The Common Ground of Wesley and Edwards." *Harvard Theological Review* 83 (1990): 271-303.

Dieter, Melin E. "John Wesley and Creative Synthesis." *Asbury Seminarian*. 39 (1984): 3-7.

Harrington, Susan F. "Friendship Under Fire: George Whitefield and John Wesley, 1739-1741." *Andover Newton Quarterly* 15 (1975): 167-181.

Hynson, Leon O. "John Wesley: A Man for All Seasons." *Asbury Seminarian* 38 (1983): 3-17.

———. "John Wesley and the *Unitas Fratrum*: A Theological Analysis." *Methodist History* 18 (1979): 26-60.

———. "Religion and Politics, Truth and Toleration: Toward a Wesleyan Political Philosophy." *Evangelical Journal* 15 (1997): 18-32.

———. "Wesley's *Thoughts Upon Slavery*: A Declaration of Human Rights." *Methodist History* 33 (1994): 46-57.

Jacobsen, Douglas. "Purity or Tolerance: The Social Dimension of Hermeneutics in the Calvinist, Arminian and American Evangelical Traditions." *Evangelical Journal* 11 (1993): 3-20.

Jordan, Albert F. "The Chronicle of Peter Boehler." *Transactions of the Moravian Historical Society* 22 (1971).

Keefer, Luke L., Jr. "John Wesley and English Arminianism." *Evangelical Journal* 4 (1986): 15-28.

Lambert, Frank. "The Great Awakening as Artifact: George Whitefield and the Construction of Intercolonial Revival, 1739-1745." *Church History* 60 (1991): 223-246.

Lawson, Kenneth E. "Who Founded Methodism? Wesley's Dependence on Whitefield in the Eighteenth Century English Revival." *Reformation and Revival Journal* 4 (1995): 39-58.

Maddox, Randy L. "Opinions, Religion, and *Catholic Spirit*: John Wesley on Theological Integrity." *Asbury Theological Journal* 47 (1992): 63-87.

O'Malley, J. Steven. "Pietistic Influence on John Wesley: Wesley and Gerhard Tersteegen." *Wesleyan Theological Journal* 31 (1996): 48-70.

Rack, Henry D. "Religious Societies and the Origin of Methodism." *Journal of Ecclesiastical History* 38 (1987): 582-595.

Reist, Irwin W. "John Wesley and George Whitefield: A Study in the Integrity of Two Theologies of Grace." *Evangelical Quarterly* 47 (1975): 26-40.

Rowe, Kenneth E. "From Eighteenth Century Encounter to Nineteenth Century Estrangement: Images of Moravians in the Thought of Methodist Bishops Asbury and Simpson." *Methodist History* 24 (1986): 171-178.

Sloat, William A., II. "George Whitefield, African Americans, and Slavery." *Methodist History* 33 (1994): 3-13.

Smith, Timothy L. "George Whitefield and Wesleyan Perfectionism." *Wesleyan Theological Journal* 19 (1984): 63-85.

———. "John Wesley and the Wholeness of Scripture." *Interpretation* 39 (1985): 246-262.

————. "Whitefield and Wesley on Righteousness by Grace." *Theological Students Fellowship Bulletin* 9 (1986): 5-8.

Smith, Warren Thomas. "Eighteenth Century Encounters: Methodist-Moravian." *Methodist History* 24 (1986): 141-156.

Steele, Richard B. "John Wesley's Synthesis of the Revival Practices of Jonathan Edwards, George Whitefield, Nicholas von Zinzendorf." *Wesleyan Theological Journal* 30 (1995): 154-172.

Stoeffler, F. Ernest. "Religious Roots of the Early Moravian and Methodist Movements." *Methodist History* 24 (1986): 132-140.

Thomas, Howe O. "John Wesley's Awareness and Application of the Method of Distinguishing Between Theological Essentials and Theological Opinions." *Methodist History* 26 (1988): 84-97.

————. "John Wesley's Understanding of the Theological Distinction Between 'Essentials' and 'Opinions.'" *Methodist History* 33 (1995): 139-148.

Tyson, John R. "Lady Huntingdon's Reformation." *Church History* 64 (1995): 580-593.

Zehrer, Karl. "The Relationship Between Pietism in Halle and Early Methodism." *Methodist History* 17 (1979): 212-224.

Index

About the Author

James L. Schwenk is a native of Pennsylvania, living his entire life near many places where George Whitefield preached during the Great Awakening. He is a graduate of United Wesleyan College (BA), Evangelical School of Theology (Mdiv) and Drew University (Mphil and PhD). An ordained itinerant elder in the Evangelical Congregational Church, Schwenk has served as pastor in churches in Schuylkill, Berks, Lehigh, Lancaster, and Lebanon Counties in his home state. A recent Fellow of the Young Center for Anabaptist and Pietist Studies at Elizabethtown College, Schwenk currently serves as Professor of Church History at Evangelical Theological Seminary where he is also the Dean of Dech Memorial Chapel. He is an avid Formula 1 Grand Prix fan, and a collector of the works of J.R.R. Tolkien. He is married to Loretta Friends, and they have two children.